CONDITIONS
OF SURRENDER

INTERNATIONAL LIBRARY OF HISTORICAL STUDIES

SERIES ISBN 1 86064 079 6

1 Between Mars and Mammon: Colonial Armies and the Garrison State in Nineteenth-century India
Douglas Peers   1 85043 954 0

2 Empires in Conflict: Armenia and the Great Powers, 1912–1920
Manoug Somakian   1 85043 912 5

3 The Military Revolution of Sixteenth-century Europe
David Eltis   1 85043 960 5

4 Patrons and Defenders: The Saints in the Italian City-states
Diana Webb   1 86064 029 x

5 Independence or Death! British Sailors and Brazilian Independence, 1822–1825
Brian Vale   1 86064 060 5

6 Workers Against Lenin: Labour Protest and the Bolshevik Revolution
Jonathan Aves   1 86064 067 2

7 European Impact and Pacific Influence: British and German Colonial Policy in the Pacific Islands and the Indigenous Response
Hermann Hiery and John MacKenzie   1 86064 059 1

8 Conditions of Surrender: Britons and Germans Witness the End of the War
Ulrike Jordan   1 86064 100 8

9 Gentlemen Capitalists: British Imperialism in Southeast Asia 1770–1890
Anthony Webster   1 86064 171 7

10 Governed by Opinion: Politics, Religion and the Dynamics of Communication in Stuart London, 1637–1645
Dagmar Freist   1 86064 110 5

11 The New British History: Founding a Modern State, 1500–1707
Glenn Burgess   1 86064 190 3

12 Pilgrims and Pilgrimage in Medieval Europe
Diana Webb   1 86064 191 1

13 The Politics of Diplomacy: Britain, France and the Balkans in the First World War
David Dutton   1 86064 112 1

15 The Right in France: Nationalism and the State, 1789–1996
Nicholas Atkin and Frank Tallatt   1 86064 197 0

CONDITIONS OF SURRENDER

Britons and Germans Witness
the End of the War

Edited by
ULRIKE JORDAN

BLOOMSBURY ACADEMIC
LONDON • NEW YORK • OXFORD • NEW DELHI • SYDNEY

BLOOMSBURY ACADEMIC
Bloomsbury Publishing Plc
50 Bedford Square, London, WC1B 3DP, UK
1385 Broadway, New York, NY 10018, USA
29 Earlsfort Terrace, Dublin 2, Ireland

BLOOMSBURY, BLOOMSBURY ACADEMIC and the Diana logo
are trademarks of Bloomsbury Publishing Plc

First published in Great Britain by Tauris Academic Studies 1997
An imprint of I.B. Tauris
Paperback edition published by Bloomsbury Academic 2021

Copyright © Ulrike Jordan, 1997

Ulrike Jordan has asserted her right under the Copyright,
Designs and Patents Act, 1988, to be identified as Author of this work.

For legal purposes the Acknowledgements on p. vii constitute
an extension of this copyright page.

All rights reserved. No part of this publication may be reproduced or
transmitted in any form or by any means, electronic or mechanical,
including photocopying, recording, or any information storage or retrieval
system, without prior permission in writing from the publishers.

Bloomsbury Publishing Plc does not have any control over, or responsibility for,
any third-party websites referred to or in this book. All internet addresses given
in this book were correct at the time of going to press. The author and publisher
regret any inconvenience caused if addresses have changed or sites have
ceased to exist, but can accept no responsibility for any such changes.

A catalogue record for this book is available from the British Library.

A catalog record for this book is available from the Library of Congress.

ISBN: HB: 978-1-8606-4100-8
PB: 978-1-3501-8317-9

Typeset by Lucy Morton, London SE12

To find out more about our authors and books visit
www.bloomsbury.com and sign up for our newsletters.

Contents

Acknowledgements vii

Preface
Peter Wende ix

Introduction
Ulrike Jordan 1

PART I

1 British Post-War Planning for Germany:
   Haunted by the Past
   Lothar Kettenacker 13

2 The German 'National Character' in British
   Perspective
   Anthony J. Nicholls 26

3 'A Mixture of Stubborn Resistance and Sudden
   Surrender': The British Media Report on the End
   of the War in Europe
   Ulrike Jordan 40

4 Towards Occupation: First Encounters in North
   Germany
   Kurt Jürgensen 53

PART II

5	Fifty Years On: Accounts by Eyewitnesses	69
6	Extracts from Contemporary Correspondence and Diaries	87
7	Contemporary Documents and Broadcasts	114
8	Statistics	148
	Select Bibliography	152
	Notes on Contributors	159
	Index	161

Acknowledgements

This volume would not have been possible without the invaluable support of many people. In early 1994, the idea for a symposium on the end of the Second World War grew out of discussions at the German Historical Institute. From the start, its director Peter Wende encouraged both the conference project and the present publication in every possible way, and I would like to extend my sincere gratitude to him for both academic and institutional support. Also, thanks are due to all the participants at the symposium on 4 May 1995, who in their contributions and discussions laid the foundation for this book.

Lothar Kettenacker, Deputy Director of the German Historical Institute London, was – as always – of great help and support in discussing both the general concept and specific aspects of the publication. For the collection of source material I drew on the expertise of many librarians and scholars. In particular I would like to thank Irina Renz (Bibliothek für Zeitgeschichte) and Stephen Walton (Imperial War Museum). Every effort has been made to obtain permission to reproduce extracts from correspondence and diaries held by these libraries. In cases where this proved impossible, the archives have granted permission *in absentia* to use this material. Crown copyright material in the Public Record Office is reproduced by permission of Her Majesty's Stationery Office. Photographs are reproduced by courtesy of the trustees of the Imperial War Museum. Lastly, I would like to express great thanks to my friends and colleagues Jane Rafferty and Angela Davies, without whose expertise in editing and translation this volume would not have come together.

Ulrike Jordan,
London, October 1996

Preface

The idea for this volume grew out of a symposium organized by the German Historical Institute London. 'Conditions of Surrender: Britons and Germans Witness the End of the War in 1945' was held to mark the fiftieth anniversary of 4 May 1945, the day when German forces surrendered to British troops in northern Germany.

The impact of the past is always present. Unfortunately, we tend to remember it only on anniversaries, which operate by dates. Historians must not ignore them, but they should try to take control and offer guidelines, so that stage-managed acts of collective remembrance are not put at the disposal of one-sided and short-lived political objectives.

Remembering as an attempt to conserve the past is the beginning of all history. But just as collective memory transcends the sum of the memories of individuals, so history, gained in critical dialogue with tradition, transcends collective memory.

The present volume brings together contemporary evidence, personal recollections, and scholarly assessment. It concentrates on what is probably the most important turning point so far in the long and eventful history of Anglo-German relations. May 1945 marked the transition from decades of conflict to an era of peace and co-operation. Focusing on this decisive historical event from different angles may provide a starting point for discussion of its wider implications. These go as far as the controversial issue of whether Germans nowadays should celebrate liberation or mourn defeat.

There are many people to thank. We are grateful to the participants in the stimulating event that provided the starting point for the present volume. Thanks are also due to the Imperial War Museum, the Public Record Office and the Bibliothek für Zeitgeschichte, Stuttgart, for providing the source material reproduced here. But, most of all, thanks must go to Ulrike Jordan for all her hard work in putting this volume together.

Peter Wende
London, February 1996

Introduction
ULRIKE JORDAN

> Our guns fired the last salvo at 8 a.m. I suppose we shall have to fight another war on the political front. God knows how we are going to save any of Germany from the results of her criminal folly.[1]

This comment by a British officer and medical doctor, made in northern Germany on 5 May 1945, presents the key themes of the immediate post-surrender period: survival in the midst of destruction and emergence from mental disorientation. Crucial in both instances were encounters between victors and vanquished. These encounters between Germans and Britons in the spring of 1945, ranging from military confrontation and first aid for civilians to the building up of an administration and the bare bones of a new infrastructure in defeated Germany, are the theme of this book.

The last days of April and the first weeks of May 1945 in Germany were indeed a period of getting to know each other in the circumstances of unconditional surrender, which in itself was a historical novelty: victors and vanquished met for the first time, carrying all the burdens of propaganda-instilled ideas of 'the other'. This situation was greatly exacerbated for the German population during these weeks by the grave problems of survival. The unique situation in which the Allies took over 'supreme authority', officially pronounced on 5 June 1945, was, in these early days, experienced at the local level as a transfer of power in chaotic circumstances. Its consequences and the structures of occupation policy were as yet unknown, and there was an atmosphere of widespread disorientation which lasted throughout spring 1945. Allied expectations of resistance, based on their wartime analysis of the German mentality and morale, were not fulfilled by actual experience.

The German population, in a reaction of resignation and relief, did not present the expected large-scale threat in the shape of the dreaded 'Werewolf' resistance movements. Instead, German reactions to defeat (the title of one of the British documents included in this volume) oscillated between a numbness towards any political and moral responsibility and the sheer struggle for survival in a society 'on the move' from East to West, from concentration camp to temporary shelter, from evacuation to an uncertain home, and from totalitarianism to occupation. The entire Nazi elite, on the other hand, including Hitler and his last entourage, had extricated themselves from responsibility either by suicide or flight. Only the 'Hitler myth', a phenomenon recognized both by post-war researchers on Nazi Germany and by contemporary foreign observers, held some, mostly short-lived, fascination for Germans in 1945.

This volume looks more closely at the transition period around capitulation in April–May 1945. What were the conditions of surrender, experienced by Germans and Britons alike? What was the reaction of contemporaries during the weeks and days before and after the capitulation? Was it utter relief at the end of hostilities, and some degree of moral justification on the part of the Allies, and dejection, stubborn resistance and ideological entrenchment on the German side? The psychological implications of this crucial time between the end of April and the first week of May 1945 were decisive. They were important not only in terms of future relations between vanquished and victors; they also mirrored long-standing wartime interpretations of the other side. Propaganda, clichés, fighting morale and indoctrination did not vanish from people's minds within a fortnight. The signing of the capitulations gave formal authority to the Allied Supreme Command and created the backdrop against which psychological change occurred.

But this proved to be an extremely slow process. Any attempt to deal with its beginnings, therefore, must look closely at its preconditions and at early signs of the persistence or transformation of ideological and propaganda-instilled notions. A first step in approaching this process is to identify long-established clichés that were exacerbated by popular presentations in the media. A second step is to turn to the practical situational changes in the time around capitulation that affected people's behaviour and thinking patterns in an almost subconscious, inevitable way in their dealings with 'the other'. This volume attempts to do this, focusing strongly on the grassroots perspective of the contemporary soldier and civilian. The approach comprises four avenues of analysis and perception: scholarly essays are supplemented by eyewitness accounts, extracts from contemporary correspondence, official documents and statistical material.

The focus on the immediate post-surrender period promises to be fruitful, since it has not received much attention from historians. On the German side, sources are few and far between due to the destruction of war, disruption of public services and wilful elimination of records by the Nazis. Yet the juxtaposition of these records, which predominantly show the dogged persistence of propaganda, with official and private Allied documents provides an opportunity to assess both the confrontational and the conciliatory aspects of the first encounters between victors and vanquished. This attempt seems all the more important in the light of the gap that exists between the high-profile character of public acts of remembrance and the dearth of historical analysis.

While the contributions to this volume deal with the preconditions and consequences of the German capitulation, its legal, social and psychological implications, and the impressions it left on the psyche of contemporaries, they presuppose, of necessity, knowledge of large parts of the historical background against which these interactions and changes occurred. As the following sketch will show, these events had gathered momentum since the early days of 1945.

The new year, after speeches by Goebbels and Hitler, which oscillated between euphoria and gloom, had already witnessed devastating events for Germany. On 13 January 1945, Soviet troops crossed the German border in east Prussia. Some months before, in autumn 1944, Anglo-American units had already reached Western German territory. Everywhere German troops had to go onto the defensive, after the disastrous results of the Ardennes offensive, Hitler's last desperate military manoeuvre. From January 1945, everyday life was a shambles. Public services (railways, mail) were disrupted and the scarcity of some foodstuffs produced a psychological climate of uprootedness. While refugees started to trek westward on a massive scale, civilians in all parts of Germany had to cope with the high level of destruction in their cities. News of military defeat on the western, southern and eastern fronts coincided with the collapse of order within Germany. February brought further advances by the Russian, American and British troops. By April, the decisive encirclement of Berlin by Soviet units had begun, and Soviet and American forces had met at Torgau, on the Elbe.

Indeed, the war had reached its final stage by late April. There was no longer one theatre of war for the German troops, but a northern and a southern theatre, with additional fighting in the east. Inside Germany, the mobilization of the so-called *Volkssturm* (people's army), consisting entirely of Hitler Youth members and old-age pensioners, cynically perverted the idea of social community and its ideology of live or die. Meanwhile, Hitler, increasingly recognizing the inevitability of the end, had, in a chaotic and controversial process, arranged for Admiral Karl Dönitz to become Reich President and Supreme Commander of the Wehrmacht (testament of 29 April 1945). On the afternoon of 30 April, Hitler committed suicide in the bunker of the Reich Chancellery, together with Eva Braun, and after an interregnum of about a day, Dönitz was notified of the contents of Hitler's will. The short period of the last Nazi government began, amidst frantic northward movements by the Supreme Command's headquarters.

The German Reich government finally ceased to exist with the arrest of Dönitz and his ramshackle cabinet on 23 May, but separate military capitulations, most importantly by the chief of the German navy, Admiral General von Friedeburg, to Field Marshal Montgomery at Lüneburg heath on 4 May, had already signalled the reality of final military defeat. Faced with unrelenting Allied demands for total military surrender to Allied troops, Alfred Jodl, chief of the Wehrmacht's supreme command, signed the military capitulation of Germany in Reims on 7 May, at 2.41 a.m. This was followed by separate signings by the chief of the supreme command of the Wehrmacht, Wilhelm Keitel, chief of the war navy, Hans-Georg von Friedeburg, and the chief commander of the Reich air force, Hans-Jürgen Stumpff, in the Soviet Headquarters in Berlin on 8–9 May. The Germans were told of the capitulation on the radio on 7 May at 12.45 p.m. Thus conditions in Germany in May 1945 can be described as insecure. There was an atmosphere of anxiety, and people in the East feared the Red Army's revenge for German atrocities committed in the Soviet Union. But there was also fear of the Western Allies' attitude towards the Germans. Bombed-out, devastated, out of reach of relatives and prisoners-of-war, the majority of Germans suffered a psychological condition that mirrored outward circumstances.

The occupying forces of the British Army also experienced a mixture of horror and pity. Apart from the scenes of devastation and the taking of prisoners-of-war, there were issues that transcended the experience of warfare in history. The sight of the concentration camps Bergen-Belsen, Buchenwald, Sandbostel and others shocked the liberators deeply and influenced their perception of and attitude towards the occupied country. The immediate impact of unconditional surrender produced stark encounters in a temporary wasteland.

The essays and selections of material in this volume deal with different facets of this time of transition between mid-April and mid-May 1945, and provide a varied methodological approach: historical analysis, eyewitness accounts, correspondence, photographs and official source material. It should be pointed out that the British point of view predominates because of the diverse role the British were to assume as victors, occupiers, helpers and – given time – partners of the Federal Republic. It is also a result of the fact that not many sources for the immediate post-surrender period have survived in Germany. The postal services were increasingly interrupted during spring 1945, and the uprootedness of life for many Germans is reflected in the records we have today. While the British view is clearly the dominant perspective, the more passive perceptions and reactions of members of the German army and the civilian population are also taken into account wherever possible.

Chapter 1 deals with the dichotomy between popular images coloured by war and propaganda and long-term, rational post-war planning in the pre-surrender period. Following up these basic themes, subsequent chapters analyse continuities and changes in preconceptions in the fields of popular representation (media) and practical politics. The main area under investigation is northern Germany. Thus we can take a fresh look at issues such as the antifraternization policy and other basic tenets of British occupation policy with the benefit of hindsight. The first four chapters work together in presenting May 1945 not so much as a watershed in politics and images, as 'zero hour', but more as a subtle turning point in mutual perceptions. Different though these assessments might be, they are bound together by their common emphasis on the transitional phase between late April and early May 1945. Although this was a decisive moment in people's lives, it has not so far received much attention from scholars or the media looking back at the end of the war.

Lothar Kettenacker's contribution (Chapter 1) analyses the pre-surrender premisses of British policies for Germany. It concentrates on the discrepancies between wartime planning and post-war reality. Having witnessed the aftermath of the First World War, the generation of British politicians and civil servants who were responsible for future occupation policy at that time were almost obsessed with events after 1918. Seen in this light, their planning for Germany was a way of coming to terms with the past. It went without saying that the Nazi regime must be removed, but in the long term the real challenge was to get rid of Germany's power potential, and to discredit Prussian militarism and power politics. Thus two conclusions were reached which were never called into question: first, that there would be no compromise peace with a successor regime led by the Wehrmacht; second, that the intention was to occupy the whole of Germany. Thus all plans were based on the assumption that there would be unconditional surrender.

Occupation and joint control by the Allies also served another purpose: it provided an incentive for continuing a wartime alliance that was both heterogeneous and fragile. The Allied Control Commission, a British idea, and special status for Berlin were the cornerstones of British planning, which was based on the time-honoured colonial principle of indirect rule. However, the success of British post-war planning depended on two preconditions which were not given in the immediate post-surrender period. First, it assumed a willingness to co-operate on the part of Stalin, who was extremely difficult to pin down and in that respect comparable to Hitler. Second, it presupposed a timely capitulation by the Wehrmacht, which, it was assumed, was still imbued with the Prussian spirit and which would not only shrug off the Nazi regime but also hand over the state apparatus intact. Kettenacker concludes that in the end the British had also become victims of Prussia's historical legend: by now Prussia was a mere shadow of its former self.

Anthony J. Nicholls picks up this theme in his chapter on the development of British ideas of the German national character (Chapter 2). He acknowledges that national character, both as a phenomenon and as a concept, is a highly complex and problematic term, but feels that it deserves historical analysis because it was so widely used in the first half of the twentieth century. He presents a historical survey which starts with the founding of Bismarck's Reich in 1871. Nicholls's differentiated portrayal of British public opinion shows clearly that the attitude towards Germany was almost universally ambivalent: on the one hand the British public rejected Germany's militarism, but on the other generally admired its cultural achievements. During both world wars the most negative images of Germany, based on exaggerated stereotypes, were bandied about in the media and in political circles. Nicholls goes on to describe the reactions among the British public, especially after the First World War, to the emergence of militarism.

The consensus regarding the German national character remained intact, although there was a phase of welcoming the progressive tendencies of the Weimar Republic. The negative views of German national character deepened during the Second World War. In the spring of 1945, it took a different turn in its effect on the British public debate. The prevailing catchword was 're-education', which covered both denazification and demilitarization. Nicholls concludes by looking ahead to the later occupation period, the origins of the Cold War coinciding with German political consolidation, and economic recovery from 1948. In his opinion, the myths of national character were increasingly discarded as common sense prevailed.

In Chapter 3 Ulrike Jordan continues the main themes of the previous chapter. She examines how the end of the war was reported in the British media. Concentrating on newspapers and BBC broadcasts, she makes three main points. She describes the British view of the German mentality, both individual and collective, as portrayed in the media, with particular emphasis on

German attitudes to Nazi policies and the regime's officials. Her look at a cross-section of the daily press reveals that by spring 1945 most commentators in Britain were convinced of the Germans' collective guilt and that the 'Führer cult' was still alive. Second, she shows how Germans in Britain, particularly the prisoners-of-war and émigrés, were portrayed to the British reader and listener. There was more differentiation, and opinions were less influenced by the immediate impressions of the last few weeks of the war. For instance, the many worthwhile and positive contributions made by German émigrés to British public and academic life were valued highly. Finally, Jordan addresses the interpretations offered by the media of the years since 1933. Newspaper columns tended to be dominated by stereotyped views of the German national character (militaristic, mystical, and so on), while BBC radio broadcasts largely reported events 'as they happened'.

Chapter 4, by Kurt Jürgensen, concentrates on the practical side of encounters between Britons and Germans at the end of the war. His analysis of the end of hostilities in northern Germany centres on the first encounters between victors and vanquished. This meant the confrontation between Montgomery's 21st Army group and the Wehrmacht units on the brink of capitulation on the one hand, and on the other the dialogue between the British Military Government detachments and the German authorities. Admiral von Friedeburg's signing of the instrument of surrender marked not only the end of the war, but, according to Jürgensen, also the dawn of a new era in Anglo-German relations.

On the British side there was the intention to build a new democratic and peaceable society from the ruins. This involved the reorientation of the German people on a grand scale, even if, as Jürgensen points out, the concept of 're-education' with its patronizing connotations was as much a taboo for the British occupation force as it was for the Germans themselves.

Jürgensen illustrates the very first contacts between Britons and Germans and gives a number of examples. All in all, these show that British reactions to post-war Germans and the conditions they found on occupying the country were governed at all times by a balance of interests. A case in point is their relationship with the Dönitz government. The British granted it a remarkably free hand in organizing the westward movement of German troops and civilian refugees to the British Zone. If this policy at the highest level is one illustration of the principle of indirect rule, another is the fact that the occupying forces initially left the Prussian administrative machinery in Schleswig-Holstein intact.

Moving on to the early days and weeks of occupation, Jürgensen describes the British attitude towards the German population and also the German authorities as 'just, but firm and distant'. Practical necessity dictated that personnel decisions were largely governed by what was needed for an efficient administration. This led to compromises in, for example, purging compromised German officials and removing them from their posts. Finally, Jürgensen points out that the priority of British policy in Germany was to instil the idea of democracy in the Germans. This was to be achieved in the most informal way possible, and not by indiscriminately transplanting British institutions to Germany. The British military governor regarded his main task, after military victory, as winning the 'battle of the mind'. In this, according to Jürgensen, he was successful.

So we return to the initial questions about long-lived clichés and ideas of 'national character' on both the British and the German side. Did the watershed of 1945, often described as anything but 'zero hour', break up these ideas as a result of encounters between Germans and Britons? Documents assembled in Part II of this volume attempt to shed more light on these questions.

The statements presented in Chapter 5 comprise recent accounts by contemporary eyewitnesses who experienced the end of the war in uniform, fighting on one or the other side of the conflict. These contributions, composed after fifty years, add the dimension of hindsight and long-term personal analysis to the experiences they describe. By contrast, the extracts from contemporary correspondence contained in Chapter 6 reflect a commentary on the situation aimed at a private readership, written immediately and often without time for reflection. These letters, all written between the last fighting and the impact of capitulation, are mostly by ordinary members of the British Army or the Wehrmacht, or by civilians on both sides. These letters reflect various aspects of the chaos and utter horror of these weeks. Most importantly, they reveal British and German reactions to the discovery of concentration camps, not only Bergen-Belsen, but also smaller camps like Sandbostel. Thus the perspective of the liberator is contrasted with that of the downcast witness. They touch upon questions of collective guilt and other moral issues, as well as describing day-to-day life and the hardships of military conditions. The same is true for the selection of photographs, a choice of documentation which again reflects the main themes of the volume: from final military operations such as securing prisoners-of-war and crossing the river Elbe, to the discovery of concentration camps and the first crucial encounters between British soldiers and German civilians around the time of the announcement of the capitulation on 8 May 1945.

Each category of sources – both the contemporary accounts and those with the benefit of hindsight – brings its own specific problems to historical analysis. In addition to subjectivity and limited perspective, which is at least potentially common to both, the contemporary letter tends to give a self-centred view, whereas the commentary after fifty years might suffer from the demonstration of retrospective knowledge and judgements not available at the time. Nevertheless, both types of source undoubtedly offer unique opportunities to help put together the puzzle of historical mentalities.

Chapter 7 provides a selection of documents which originated in the British Foreign Office. They pick up the thread of propaganda, information and observation, as well as preparation for occupation, introduced in the essays. Topics range from 'The mentality of the German officer' to the lengthy analysis of 'German reactions to defeat' and German broadcasts around the time of capitulation. Following on from this, Chapter 8 provides statistical overviews related to the Second World War. Finally, a bibliographical essay and an index end the volume. It is hoped that this book will contribute to each individual reader's assessment of the key issues relating to 'unconditional surrender': pre-formed opinions, expectations, experiences shared and hardships experienced in the spring of 1945.

NOTES

1. Captain Robert Barer MC, Correspondence, 5 May 1945, Imperial War Museum, London, Department of Documents.

Part I

I

British Post-War Planning for Germany: Haunted by the Past

LOTHAR KETTENACKER

The events of 1989–90 have reminded us that historians are no wiser than others in predicting the future. German academics were among the most outspoken in dismissing the nation-state in the name of peace and progress.[1] All of a sudden, the German nation-state has resurfaced on the map of Europe. Does it mean that the past has caught up with us? The calling of the historian is to try to make sense of the past; of what, at face value, appears to be sheer nonsense. I shall try to elaborate on two themes: first, that history does not repeat itself; and second, that it does, nevertheless, have a meaning which is bound to shape our consciousness.

John Maynard Keynes for one was perfectly aware of the fundamental difference between history and politics. Scathing about the folly of Versailles as early as 1919, he warned in 1944: 'The chief thing that matters is that ministers should not suppose that the chief thing that matters is to avoid the mistakes made last time.'[2] Now the consequences of the peace were there for all to see. Versailles had been Hitler's most effective propaganda weapon in the 1920s and the clue to his foreign policy successes in the 1930s. Hence, avoiding the mistakes made at Versailles was uppermost in the minds of British policy-makers in the Second World War. This time they would do a better job and make sure that both the Nazi regime and the old Prussian elite would be crushed. As a result, new mistakes were made. May 1945 did not mark *finis Germaniae*, as Hitler hoped to stage-manage,[3] nor the demise merely of the Führer-state of 1933, but the definite end of the Bismarck Reich of 1871. The very misconception on which British post-war planning was based only serves to prove that the old Germany, dominated by Prussia, had already been destroyed from within before its armies surrendered unconditionally.

Among the three major Allies, Britain took the lead in preparing the agenda for the end of hostilities. To some extent, diplomacy had to compensate for military setbacks and a growing gap in manpower and material resources between Britain and her new Allies, Soviet Russia and the United States of America. When Stalin had asked for twenty-five to thirty divisions following Britain's offer of assistance on 12 July 1941, Churchill dismissed his demand as 'a physical absurdity'.[4] Nor was Britain ready for a second front as early as the Russians and Americans had pressed for. However, when Britain concluded a formal alliance with the Soviet Union on 26 May 1942, the government had reason to hope that London was in an ideal position to remain one of the big players, by acting as the mediator between the new superpowers.[5] The tacit assumption was that America and Russia would provide the muscle, arms and men, and Britain would supply the brainwork. Britain saw herself as the centre, the chief manager of a growing alliance against Hitler. For this reason, the government had refrained from specifying any war aims which might cause dissension among the Allies. As early as 9 October 1939 the cabinet had come to the conclusion: 'We should avoid any precise statement of our war aims.'[6] Churchill in particular approved of this principle and tried to adhere to it throughout the war.

Eden's visit to Moscow in December 1941 is a good example of the pitfalls of specific war aims. The Foreign Secretary, arriving empty-handed, was greatly tempted to fall in with Stalin's main demand, recognition of the Soviet Union's western border as agreed between Ribbentrop and Molotov. He was only prevented from doing so by intense diplomatic pressure from Washington, notably Foreign Secretary Cordell Hull.[7] The lesson was clear: progress could be made only by shelving all controversial issues and pursuing a technocratic approach. This was, anyway, Whitehall's favourite procedure for solving problems between ministers of different political persuasions. The inter-ministerial committee system was now grafted on to the inter-Allied decision-making process. In spite of Churchill's misgivings, early planning for the end of the war was deemed to be essential, mainly for two reasons: first, lack of preparation was regarded as one of the chief causes of the failure of the Versailles Treaty; second, a scramble for Germany by the victorious powers towards the end of the war had to be avoided at all costs.

With virtually no political direction from above, early planning would make sense only on the basis of certain assumptions. The most important of these were not arrived at after long cabinet deliberations, or the result of memoranda put down by Whitehall mandarins. They were, in other words, foregone conclusions: there should be no compromise peace, not only because it was unlikely to find favour with the United States and Soviet Russia; not only because bargaining over terms would make any advance planning so much more difficult; but because it meant that German military potential would only be weakened, as in 1918, not removed for good. The principle of unconditional surrender, then, had been established long before Roosevelt made it public at the Conference of Casablanca early in 1943. In his official history of British foreign policy in the Second World War, Sir Llewellyn Woodward states categorically: 'The British discussion on the treatment of Germany after the war assumed an unconditional surrender, and took no account of the possibility of bargaining over terms.'[8] Indeed, no other conclusion is possible now that the source material has been made available. Hitler and the Nazi regime were not the only enemy. At the end of the war they would disappear as a matter of course, like the Kaiser and the Hohenzollern monarchy. However, it was equally important that the old Prussian-German ruling elite, which had given Hitler a helping hand in preparing for war, should be wholly discredited and deprived of power. As Churchill put it on 21 September 1943: 'Nazi tyranny *and* Prussian militarism are the two main elements in German life which must be absolutely destroyed. They must be absolutely rooted out if Europe and the world are to be spared a third and still more frightful conflict.'[9] In the same speech he then referred to the 'twin roots of all our evils', which 'must be extirpated'. Occupation of the whole of Germany was therefore called for in order to prevent any new stab-in-the-back legend and to drive home to every German in the remotest corner of the country that war did not pay. There was no shortage of bourgeois or social-democratic émigrés in London pointing out that most Nazi leaders were not of Prussian origin. But this was immaterial to British planning staffs, who argued that the army, the civil service and the leading industrialists had been moulded by the Prussian spirit, and that without their willing collaboration Hitler would never have dared to challenge the world and start another war.

Early in the war Robert Vansittart had warned against the illusion of just fighting Hitler. The real enemy was 'Prussianism, supercharged by Nazism.'[10] Those among Eden's advisers at the Foreign Office who opposed a policy of deliberate dismemberment of Germany, as recommended by the Big Three, argued strongly in favour of partitioning Prussia instead.[11] One important argument was that the dissolution of Prussia would be popular in the west and south of Germany, whereas the destruction of Germany beyond the necessary decentralization of power might well rekindle the flames of nationalism and produce another Führer. The British educated elite believed very firmly in what had been labelled 'the Prussian myth of history', as though it had been Prussia's mission to unite Germany and to mould it in its own image. One might argue that the ghost of Prussia was more alive in Whitehall during the war than in the German High Command. Churchill, who was an old romantic, wished to reinstate the old Prussia, though without her nineteenth-century acquisitions, that is, the modern power-base of the industrial heartland of the Ruhr.[12] From a British point of view it was no farfetched assumption that, as in 1918, the army generals, true to their Prussian ethos, would know when the time had come to get rid of Hitler and sue for peace. All British and, subsequently, Allied plans were based on this scenario: the Germany army, or else a German government purged of all Nazi elements, would hand over Germany's administrative machine fully intact. That Germany would in the end be defended by a last call-up of the Hitler Youth and old-age pensioners was just too melodramatic to make sense. Again and again the British made the mistake of allowing national traditions, underpinned by common sense, to prevail in a society that was held together by irrational beliefs and sheer terror. One important clue was supplied by the constant rumours of the alleged readiness of certain German army circles to purchase a compromise peace at the cost of eliminating Hitler and replacing him by a more moderate government.

The first cabinet memorandum on the future of Germany, of 8 March 1943,[13] had been triggered by intelligence reports that Schacht, von Papen and other members of the German *Herrenclub* were forming an alternative government that would emerge after an armistice offer. The British attitude to such developments was: 'The generals must act before we talk.'[14] For more than six months the government was in two minds about whether to recognize a central government or to deal only with regional or provincial authorities. German experts drafted into the government favoured decentralization right from the start, whereas the more conservative mandarins, especially in the Treasury, preferred to transact business with a central government in Berlin. Broadly speaking, the left welcomed modernization through social upheaval; the right feared chaos and revolutionary turmoil.[15] On 5 October 1943, the cabinet approved the existing plans for an Allied Control Commission. Officials were quite certain in their own minds that Germany would remain intact as an administrative entity that could be controlled from above by a small Allied control staff. Past experience had shown that even a prostrate Germany was potentially dangerous. That is why Russia would be induced to co-operate after the war.

The events of 20 July 1944 did not come as a surprise, except in the sense that a coup had been predicted many times but had so far never materialized. When it failed, Churchill distanced himself from the plotters in words for which German historians such as Gerhard Ritter and Hans Rothfels have never forgiven him. 'The highest personalities in the German Reich are murdering one another, or trying to, while the avenging armies of the Allies close upon the doomed and ever-narrowing circle of their power.'[16] And he concluded: 'Therefore, potent as may be these manifestations of internal disease, decisive as they may be one of these days, it is not in them that we should put our trust but in our own strong arms and the justice of our cause.' The message was clear, addressed both to the Russians and Americans: we are not in collusion with these men. We have no trust in the Junker generals and the Prussian nobility; they too would have to surrender unconditionally because it is they who have forged and run the devastating German war machine. Still, Churchill's words also indicate that the Prime Minister believed the army generals had enough sense and strength to get rid of Hitler and surrender before the Reich was totally devastated. Officials, however, were less hopeful about another uprising and to some extent they were relieved that the war could now proceed according to plan, that is, without any further diplomatic complications. But they did begin to wonder whether there would be any central government or administration left to be controlled and guided from above.

By that time the Russians and Americans had already agreed to the British proposals for zones of occupation and a separate Berlin zone as the headquarters of the Allied Control Commission.[17] Only now, with the prospect of a fight to the bitter end, did the Foreign Office raise the question: 'Will Germany "go communist" after the war?' According to a distillation of comments the worst scenario was 'Germany going over to Russian communism (that is, taking orders from Moscow), or a non-communist Germany run by a clandestine party of revenge, leaning on Russia.'[18] Apparently it did not occur to British officials that the Germans were not at all inclined to trust the Russians, whose land they had devastated, or the Bolsheviks, against whom Goebbels had railed for the last three years. The hopes and fears of ordinary Germans did not figure prominently in any British plans. Occupation and control – if at all possible joint Allied control – was now all the more important to prevent total chaos, from which only the communists could benefit.

The clash between the Prime Minister and Whitehall brings into focus the problematic nature of the bureaucratic approach to politics, of what is sometimes referred to as 'the official mind'. Churchill was most sceptical about long-term planning by officials on the basis of some unproven hypotheses, but he did not put his foot down. Rather he preferred to make cynical quips. When, in October 1942, the Foreign Office produced its Four-Power Plan for ruling the post-war world, he commented: 'We shall not overlook Mrs Glass's Cooking Book recipe for jugged hare! First catch your hare!'[19] Nor was he ever a member of one of the cabinet committees dealing with requirements after cessation of hostilities. While military details exercised a great fascination for him – he was, after all, a soldier by profession – he was bored by problems connected with the future peace. 'There will be plenty of time to go into that when we have won the war', he used to say to his physician.[20]

Not surprisingly, the future of Germany was rarely discussed by the cabinet. Most of Churchill's advisers did not approve of his insistence on first things first. From their point of view the Prime Minister was short-sighted and the future had to be mapped out as far as possible. In fact, Churchill was wiser than most of his advisers and his scepticism about the policy of predetermination was fully justified. One might criticize him today for not realizing how much his scope for action at the end of the war had been curtailed by the efforts of his own government. His note to Eden of 4 January 1945 reads like a verdict on his cabinet colleagues: 'Guidance in those mundane matters is granted to us only step by step, or at the utmost a step or two ahead. There is therefore wisdom in reserving one's decisions as long as possible and until all facts and forces that will be potent at the moment are revealed.'[21] For Whitehall mandarins such rhetoric seemed to prove only that the Prime Minister was a man of the past who believed that most problems could be solved by a get-together of heads of state.

In the end the Nazis held on to power in Germany up to and beyond Hitler's death and the conquest of Berlin by the Red Army. Grand Admiral Carl Dönitz, the last head of state and supreme commander, was appointed by Hitler and enjoyed his full confidence. According to a Foreign Office minute of 17 May 1945: 'Dönitz and his gang are 100 per cent objectionable – Dönitz himself may be arraigned as a war criminal and his so-called "government" are as fine representatives of "Nazism and Prussian militarism" as it would be possible to find.'[22] However, Churchill and the Admiralty were quite satisfied that Dönitz's command over the high seas did gather up the remnants of the German fleet. The Prime Minister was one of the last and staunchest defenders of indirect rule. He would fight the German generals to the bitter end, but was then prepared to entrust them with authority, in the same way as Moscow used communist agents to run their zone. He had no problems with General Busch establishing his overall authority in Schleswig-Holstein, which had caused so much uproar in Allied quarters, and alarmed the Foreign Office.

Churchill was unperturbed and explained to Sir Orme Sargent, who substituted for Eden: 'We will never be able to rule Germany apart from the Germans unless you are prepared to let every miserable little school-child lay its weary head upon your already overburdened lap.'[23] In vain had he tried to persuade General Eisenhower to push across the Elbe towards Berlin. Now that the Red Army had conquered the German capital, and might set up a puppet government, he wished to hold on to the last vestiges of a legitimate government in British hands.

However, it was the well-known anti-Bolshevik tirades of the Flensburg cabinet and its unfounded hopes for an alliance with the Western Allies against Russia which contributed to its early demise. On 2 May the new German Foreign Secretary, Count Schwerin von Krosigk, let it be known over the wireless: 'Peace can be brought to the world only if the Bolshevik tidal wave does not flood Europe. In a heroic fight which knows no equal, Germany, for four years summoning her last ounce of strength, formed the bulwark of Europe and the entire world against the red flood. She could have saved Europe from Bolshevism had her rear not been menaced.'[24] This rhetoric, clearly designed to divide the alliance, did not endear the Dönitz government to the Foreign Office. *The Times* (3 May 1945) reported this speech by von Ribbentrop's successor under the headline 'Bolshevist Bogey Revived', and the Foreign Office reminded Churchill of his own warning against Prussian militarism. After one German general, General von Thoma, had approached Churchill with an offer of co-operation, Sir Orme Sargent wrote to the Prime Minister: 'We had always suspected that, as soon as Germany was defeated, the German generals would repudiate Hitler and offer their co-operation in the tasks of occupation. Nor are we surprised that they are doing so "in the spirit of Christian culture". The German generals have one purpose, to preserve or reconstitute the officer caste. In fact Prussian militarism, for which these Generals stand, is, as you yourself have said, one of "the two main elements in German life which must be absolutely destroyed".'[25] The Dönitz government aroused the deepest suspicions not only in Moscow; public opinion in the West was no less scathing about the last pathetic representatives of Hitler's obnoxious regime. After twenty-three days the Grand Admiral had outlived his usefulness. With the unceremonious arrest of the last

Reich Chancellor and his cabinet, all of them suspected war criminals, the Bismarck Reich met its inglorious end.

For Britain, 8 May marked a moral rather than a political victory. Her hopes at the beginning of the war had also been shattered. Only half of Europe had been liberated. Poland was still not a free country. The alliance with the Soviet Union of May 1942 could not prevent the onset of the Cold War, which forced Britain to take sides and abandon the hope of brokering between the new superpowers. Berlin was an empty shell, no longer the nerve centre of the Reich and suitable for the application of indirect rule through a control commission. When surveying the ruins of Berlin from the air, Harry Hopkins, President Roosevelt's special adviser, was reminded of Carthage.[26] The British zone of occupation, including Germany's industrial heartland, which had been wrested from the Americans, turned out to be more of a liability than an asset, swamped as it was by millions of refugees and cut off from the agrarian east. Sir Orme Sargent described the Ruhr area as 'the greatest heap of rubble the world has ever seen'.[27] Financially Britain was bankrupt and depended on cheap American credit. India, the jewel in the crown, was on its way to independence. And while Roosevelt's death had no adverse effect on America's leadership role, Churchill's fall from power did indeed diminish Britain's influence. After all, he, more than the country he represented, was one of the Big Three.

For Germany the break with the past was more radical than any other caesura in her history. However, the turmoil and uncertainty in May and June 1945 precluded any sober reflection on what had happened, on the true meaning of the unconditional surrender of 7 May, and the subsequent assumption of supreme authority by the victorious powers for Germany as a whole on 5 June. The mental dissociation from the past since 1871 was as much due to the efforts of German historiography as to the shocking events of 1945, necessary though they were as a prerequisite. In fact, Allied re-education was sustained beyond any expectations prevailing after the war. After all, German nationalism had not evaporated following the defeat of 1918 – why should it vanish after 1945?

British obsessions with the national character of the German people and its impact on the future are well illustrated by a cabinet memorandum of 10 January 1945 entitled 'German reactions to defeat'.[28] The author is Con O'Neill, one of the two Foreign Office advisers on Germany. He argued that National Socialism would be perceived as a 'colossal failure, but not necessarily militarism'. The latter was supposed to be inherent in the German mentality, not just the result of German history since 1871. 'National Socialism has been no more than a special form of organization of the instincts and capacities of the German people. Other forms of totalitarian organization, almost equally unpleasant and effective, may occur, for these instincts and capacities will remain largely what they are.' Such ideas were so prevalent among the British ruling elite, even those like Con O'Neill who were basically well-disposed towards the German people, that it makes no sense to attribute them just to Vansittart and a certain lunatic fringe. We can assume that many of O'Neill's colleagues shared his views. The great majority of Germans, the author maintained, 'do not think of the action of the state as being a reflection of their own wills. They prefer that it should circumscribe and define the limits within which their individual wills may act. They are therefore, in the political sense, irresponsible: they reject the burden and duty of choice. Thus there can be no hope for liberalism in Germany.'

It would be unjust to dismiss such a perception as pure nonsense. Anyone who remembered how easily Hitler had swept to power and then kept seeing clips of newsreels, showing how the Führer was idolized and obeyed, could not help feeling that 'the German mass insists on abdication'. Con O'Neill speculated on future German recollections of the war, which he based on the assumption that the Germans might well return to the same state of mind as after 1918. Whatever one might think of the German character, here the author certainly got it wrong: 'They will remember how near they came to victory. They will remember the battles they won, the countries they struck down, the heroes who led in success or perished in the hour of seeming triumph. Nothing will stop them from believing that they had the finest army in the world, which succumbed only to superiority in numbers and material.'

Quite a few veterans probably did just that when they gathered in pubs and got carried away by reminiscences of the war.

But German historiography pointed in the opposite direction. The self-serving memoirs of German generals and field marshals did not fool public opinion. That the army generals should have been unable to get rid of Hitler and save Germany from destruction and division by a timely surrender did much to discredit the Prussian military tradition. In fact, the generals, always rumoured to be ready for a putsch, had helped Hitler to come to power, carried out, however reluctantly, every one of his orders, and kept the war machine going to the very end. What is remembered is not any 'last ditch heroism', as Hitler and Goebbels would have it, but the stupidity of blindly following a madman up to and beyond his own destruction.

O'Neill's memorandum was a contribution to the vexing question, debated at the Foreign Office, as to whether Germany was likely to turn east or west. The main motive behind his paper was not a plea for harsh treatment of the German people. On the contrary, he argued that the inclinations of the German people, their political and social ideas and instincts, would align them with the east rather than the west, not least because Russia was in a position to restore the lost territories. However, Eden was not persuaded that the Germans were bound to side with the east. Indeed, all available evidence tended to contradict this gloomy forecast. He is likely to have been more attracted to Con O'Neill's suggestion that the Germans should be encouraged to focus their abundant energies on improving their own society, rather than imposing themselves on other countries in the pursuit of power politics: 'Germany must be encouraged to aim at being a super-Sweden, cleaner, better planned and healthier than any State ever was before, with better social, medical and educational services and a higher standard of living than any State ever had.'

What, at the time, sounded like wishful thinking in the extreme proved to become the real agenda of the future. It requires the constant vigilance of historians to make sure that Hitler will never be moved into the national pantheon, as happened to Napoleon; that the Führer-myth will not be laid to rest next to Kaiser Barbarossa in the Cyffhäuser, where the Reich has now been buried for good. Roosevelt, for one, was quite determined that the Reich should never be revived. As Klaus Hildebrand put it in his 1993 Annual Lecture to the German Historical Institute: 'The year 1945 witnessed the end of something which had started seventy-five years before. The Reich had passed away.'[29] And so has the ambition of the German people once again to play a major role in world affairs.

NOTES

1. See, for example, Harold James and Marla Stone (eds), *When the Wall Came Down. Reactions to German Unification* (London, 1992). See also Hans-Peter Schwarz, 'Mit gestopften Trompeten. Die Wiedervereiningung Deutschlands aus der Sicht westdeutscher Historiker', *Geschichte in Wissenschaft und Unterricht* 44, 1993, pp 683–704.
2. John Maynard Keynes, *Collected Writings*, ed. Donald Moggeridge (London, 1980), vol 26, p 344.
3. See Joachim C. Fest, *Hitler* (London, 1974), pp 724–6.
4. Churchill to Cripps, 25 October 1941, in Winston S. Churchill, *The Second World War*, vol 3 (London, 1950), p 413.
5. A good example of British thinking is the so-called 'Four-Power Plan'; see Lothar Kettenacker, *Krieg zur Friedenssicherung. Die Deutschlandplanung der britischen Regierung während des Zweiten Weltkriegs* (Göttingen, 1989), pp 130–46. See also *The Memoirs of Lord Gladwyn* (London, 1972), pp 109–25.
6. War Cabinet Minutes WM 42(39)8, Public Record Office: CAB 65/1.
7. See his clear-sighted memorandum for President Roosevelt, 4 February 1942, *Foreign Relations of the United States*, 1942/III, p 510.
8. Llewellyn Woodward, *British Foreign Policy in the Second World War* (London, 1962), p 478.
9. *The War Speeches of the Rt. Hon. Winston S. Churchill*, ed. Charles Eade, vol 3 (London, 1962), p 18.
10. 'Germany's Fifth War', 8 November 1939, FO 371/22986/C19495.
11. Cf. Lothar Kettenacker, 'Preußen in der alliierten Kriegszielplanung 1939–1947', in Lothar Kettenacker et al. (eds), *Studien zur Geschichte Englands und der deutsch-britischen Beziehungen. Festschrift für Paul Kluke* (Munich, 1981), pp 281–93.
12. Cf. Churchill, *The Second World War*, vol 5, p 359. At the same time he wished to re-create 'in modern form' the Austro-Hungarian Empire.
13. WP(43)96, FO 371/34457/C2864. See also Kettenacker, *Krieg zur Friedenssicherung*, pp 161–80.
14. 'Possible Development in Germany Before, During and After Military Collapse', 17 February 1943, FO 371/34456/C1818. The same attitude prevailed towards the resistance even before the war.
15. WM(135)3, CAB 64/40.
16. *Churchill's War Speeches*, vol 3, p 203 (2 August 1944). See also Lothar Kettenacker, 'Die britische Haltung zum deutschen Widerstand während des Zweiten Weltkrieges', in Lothar Kettenacker (ed.), *The 'Other Germany' in the Second World War* (Stuttgart, 1977), pp 49–77 (includes English summary).

17. See Tony Sharp, *The Wartime Alliance and the Zonal Division of Germany* (Oxford, 1975).
18. Reproduced in Kettenacker (ed.), *The 'Other Germany'*, pp 212–17.
19. M 461/2, 18 October 1942, PREM 4/100/7.
20. Lord Moran, *Winston Churchill. The Struggle for Survival 1940–1956* (London, 1966) p 180 (September 1944).
21. M 22/5, Eden Papers (University of Birmingham), vol 10, pp 408–10.
22. Minute for Eden, 17 May 1945, F) 371/46914/C2316.
23. M 474/5, 14 May 1945, F) 371/46914/C2436.
24. English translations of last official speeches (1–8 May 1945): FO 371/46785/C2388.
25. FO 371/46877/C2216.
26. Robert E. Sherwood, *The White House Papers of Harry L. Hopkins*, vol 2 (London, 1949), p 875.
27. Quoted by Rolf Steininger, *Deutsche Geschichte 1945–1961*, vol 1 (Frankfurt am Main, 1983), p 168. This is one of the best studies of the narrative plus documentation kind on post-war Germany.
28. WP(45)18, FO 371/40791/C150. See the extract reprinted in this volume, pp 115ff.
29. Klaus Hildebrand, *Reich – Nation-State – Great Power. Reflections on German Foreign Policy 1871–1945*, The 1993 Annual Lecture of the German Historical Institute London (London, 1995), p 24. See also his new magisterial work, *Das vergangene Reich. Deutsche Außenpolitik von Bismarck bis Hitler 1871–1945* (Stuttgart, 1995).

2

The German 'National Character' in British Perspective

ANTHONY J. NICHOLLS

A British Member of Parliament, writing in the *Spectator* at the beginning of May 1945, described her sense of outrage at visiting the Buchenwald concentration camp, which had recently been liberated by Allied forces. She was shocked at the apparent lack of concern shown by the inhabitants of nearby Weimar when faced with the horrors of the camp, and ended her piece with the comment 'The Hun ambition may be foiled, but the Hun spirit still lives...' 'I have returned from Germany', she went on, 'firmly convinced that the mere establishment of democratic government for such people will not solve the problem. There is undoubtedly a deep streak of evil and sadism in the German race, such as one ought not to expect to find in a people who for generations have paid lip-service to Western culture and civilisation.... Only with extreme firmness will we eliminate the beast from the German heart.'[1] This represented one British view of the Germans at the end of the Second World War, and it was a view shared by many in the population. As I shall attempt to demonstrate, it was not confined to any particular part of the British political spectrum, left or right. But as I shall also suggest, it was always ambivalent and hedged about with reservations.

The whole concept of 'national character' is, of course, highly problematic, and I sympathize with those who would reject it altogether. However, the fact that notions about national character were widely disseminated in the first half of this century, and even seem to have affected political decision-making, does make them an object of legitimate interest to historians.

After German unification and the foundation of the German Reich in 1871, the British attitude to Germany was ambivalent, but by no means negative. The patriotic German historian Heinrich von Sybel, writing in the *Fortnightly Review* in January 1871, was able to assure his mainly Liberal British readership that German unification would be a blessing for liberalism and for European civilization.[2] He could feel fairly confident that many of them would agree with him when he pointed out that the Prussian victory over the French was a victory for a moderate, Protestant, constitutional monarchy over a dangerously unstable French nation which oscillated between ultramontane clericalism on the one hand and socialistic democracy *à la* 1793 on the other.

But Sybel was aware that Bismarck's Germany had its critics in Britain. He had to play down the militaristic aspect of the Hohenzollern monarchy, claiming that the Germans had tried to unify peacefully but had been obstructed by Habsburgs and Guelphs (Hanoverians). The Prussian army had indeed been opposed by German liberals when it seemed to be a tool of reactionary Austria. Once Bismarck had changed sides and adopted the national cause, the liberals could happily support him. The unity of France, he pointed out, had also required the use of force, as had that of England with Scotland (to say nothing of Ireland!). He also had to reassure his liberal readers that the constitution of Germany, although it was clearly more authoritarian than that of Britain, was nevertheless a remarkably liberal one, giving its citizens, as it did, the prospect of gaining experience in political life at both the *Land* and the Reich level.

Sybel's comments are interesting because they reflect his understanding of two differing attitudes among the British towards the Germans, attitudes that might well be held simultaneously even though they were contradictory. The first was a feeling of similarity – or even kinship – with the Germans which related to mutual Protestantism and historical solidarity against the threat from France. The achievements of the Enlightenment and the subsequent Romantic era in German literature and philosophy – not to mention German music – raised the prestige of German culture in Britain. Well before the end of the nineteenth century, serious-minded British university students regarded a period at a German university as an important part of their professional training. At a lower, but in many ways more important, level, the Prussian public school system was often seen as a model of its kind, and educationalists in general looked to Germany when considering reforms in Britain. The German empire was also admired for its efficient bureaucracy and its burgeoning industrial economy, especially in high-tech industries, such as chemicals and electrical engineering. It was also respected for its military power.

But the latter point touched on another aspect of the German character which constantly surfaced in Britain – the notion that the Germans had given up their role as poets and thinkers when they had been unified by the military might of Prussia. Prussia's military traditions, and her illiberal political behaviour, were seen as overriding the more pacific, democratic tendencies in southern Germany. Prussianism was regarded as intolerant, boorish, humourless – and anti-British. Already in the 1880s, one future Foreign Secretary, Joseph Austen Chamberlain, was impressed by the Anglophobia he detected in Treitschke's lectures on European history.[3] In the First World War, the official British position, which seems to have found resonance at various levels of society, was that the conflict was a struggle against Prussian militarism. One British politician who seems to have absorbed this view was Winston Churchill, who persisted in regarding Prussia as the source of German aggressiveness throughout the Second World War, despite the fact that Hitler was an Austrian and Munich described itself as the 'capital' of the Nazi movement. It was no coincidence that one Allied war aim that was actually realized after 1945 was the formal dissolution of the Prussian state, which took place on 25 February 1947. This was only a symbolic act, since by then Prussia had ceased to exist. The Prussian character was supposedly exemplified in the almost mythical figure of the Junker – a bogeyman who embodied every negative trait that a liberal Briton might find repugnant: feudal in social relations, arrogant in his personal life and aggressive in foreign affairs. The social complexities of the provinces east of the Elbe were rarely explained to the British public before 1918. Afterwards the role played by the DNVP (German National People's Party) and the east Elbian landed interests in undermining the Weimar Republic confirmed rather more thoughtful observers in the view that a socially backward and politically reactionary Prussian elite was mainly responsible for German democracy's failure and for helping Hitler into power.

However, this is to anticipate later events. After the First World War a reaction set in against what were seen as crude stereotypes of militaristic Germans used in Allied propaganda. The controversy over the Versailles Peace Treaty, most famously exemplified by Keynes in his *Economic Consequences of the Peace*, together with a revulsion against the old-fashioned balance-of-power diplomacy which had apparently led Britain into the war in the first place, led to a reconsideration of British attitudes towards Germany. Descriptions of the Western Front in novels and plays stressed the folly of war, and some illustrated the resentments felt by front soldiers towards politicians and staff officers, but they showed little rancour towards the Germans. The French, on the other hand, with whom collaboration in the war had never been entirely happy, were widely distrusted.

During the Weimar Republic, Germany was perceived by many British intellectuals as the home of progressive movements in art and architecture. German life seemed in many ways nearer to that of Britain than it did that of other European countries. The Germans were orderly, clean and hard-working.

It was against this background that Hitler came to power in Germany in January 1933. The British government was given very clear warnings by its admirable ambassador in Berlin, Horace Rumbold, about the nature of Hitler's movement and the danger of aggression from the Nazi regime.[4] But reactions to the Third Reich in Britain were mixed. The *Daily Mail*, for example, had been enthusiastically pro-Nazi since 1930. On 10 July 1933 its proprietor, Lord Rothermere, published an editorial article, 'Youth Triumphant', in which he welcomed the example the Nazis were setting to the world, and referred to the achievements of Mussolini and his young collaborators, who had made Italy 'the best-governed state in Europe'. 'I confidently expect to see', he went on, 'similar results achieved by Hitler, who has come to power at the age of 43.'[5] At almost the same time a far better informed British journalist, the correspondent of the *Daily Telegraph*, G.E.R. Gedye, who had himself recently visited the new concentration camp at Dachau, was publishing some 'Impressions of Hitler's Germany'. He described how he had been told by a German in Munich that National Socialism 'suits the Germans like a Savile Row suit an Englishman. Our people can be divided into three: one part wants to be kicked, another part to kick. These make up 90 per cent. The remaining 10 per cent looks on at the spectacle and weeps.'[6] It was a view of the Germans which was to prove tenacious in the years to come.

Generally speaking, British newspapers and politicians did not follow the informed assessments of diplomats like Rumbold, but were eager to base their views on scoop interviews with Hitler or other Nazi dignitaries. In any case, the popular press gave little coverage to Continental politics. Britain was an imperial country and the less she had to do with Europe the better. If there was going to be trouble it could be blamed on the Paris peace settlement for being unfair to the Germans over such matters as national self-determination, or the one-sided restrictions placed on German rearmament. There was very little understanding of the underlying causes of the Weimar Republic's collapse, or of the complexity of German politics. Versailles had been a favourite target for German propaganda even before Hitler came to power. Many British people had come to the conclusion that revision of the treaty was justified, and that the negative version of the German character they had received before and during the First World War was a myth.

In any case, it was claimed, Hitler had a popular mandate in Germany, and so his views had to be taken seriously. Even those commentators who, like Gedye, were horrified by the Nazi tyranny, seemed to imply in their criticism that Hitler enjoyed the warm support of the German people, ignoring the fact that he had never won a majority, even in the manifestly unfair Reichstag elections of March 1933. Anti-Nazi Germans were given little credit for their views, and it was perhaps typical that the critic of Hitler who made the most impact in London in 1939–40 was the former Nazi, Hermann Rauschning, whose vivid if fanciful accounts of his conversations with Hitler caught the imagination of press and politicians. In 1939 British opinion was shocked by the failure of attempts to conciliate Germany, but the conclusions to be drawn about the German character were initially confused.

As is well known, the British government sought, after the outbreak of the Second World War, to distinguish between Hitler's Nazis and the German people. Whereas in 1914 the war had been presented as a struggle against Prussian militarism, now Hitler and the Nazi movement were the enemy. The Prime Minister, Neville Chamberlain, rapidly made a very clear distinction between the Nazis and the German people when he talked of 'Hitler's War', and said that 'We have no quarrel with the German people except that they allow themselves to be governed by a Nazi government.' The left-wing labour politician Stafford Cripps put a widespread British view very succinctly when he wrote in *Tribune* on 15 September 1939 that 'Our enemy is Hitler and the Nazi system and not the German people.'[7]

Unlike the French, who urged an attack on *all* Germans as being equally wicked, the British establishment publicly maintained a strict division between good and bad Germans, the philistine Nazis and the heirs to Goethe or Kant. However, even at this early stage, opinions within the British Foreign Office about the nature of the German character were divided. In response to a concluding despatch from Neville Henderson, the pro-German British ambassador in Berlin, who had deplored the fact that the great qualities of the German race were 'being debauched for ends which are evil and to serve the ambitions ... of a single individual', Orme Sargent commented that 'It is really impossible to maintain that the German people are being governed by a small minority against their will.' His superior, Robert Vansittart, went even further. In a memorandum entitled 'Germany's fifth war' he claimed that just ridding Germany of Hitler would not solve the problem: 'we are fighting the German army and the German people on whom the army is based. We are fighting the *real* and not the accidental Germany.'[8]

This view, that the war was the fault of the Germans as a whole rather than just an evil political movement, gained ground steadily in the next year or two. It was fuelled by a sense of guilt over the failures of the so-called appeasement policy. The fall of France and the direct threat of invasion of Britain, together with the aerial bombardment of British towns in the winter of 1940–41, contributed to the hardening of anti-German sentiment, as of course did the assumption of prime ministerial office by Winston

Churchill, who symbolized an uncomplicated spirit of resistance to the enemy. Churchill was leading a coalition government dedicated to winning the war. Many of its Conservative ministers had been anti-appeasers with little time for the Germans. The minister responsible for propaganda, Brendan Bracken, brushed aside suggestions that the British should play on divisions within the German military leadership by saying, 'It is too late for redemption. They are all tarred with the same brush.'[9]

Nor were the Labour members of the coalition particularly inclined to be soft on the Germans. Clement Attlee, the deputy prime minister, believed that German militarism was as dangerous as National Socialism. In July 1943 he submitted a memorandum to the cabinet urging that, even if the Nazis were to be overthrown or liquidated by the Germans, Prussian militarism – the Junkers and their cliques – and the masters of heavy industry would have to be eliminated. Hugh Dalton, who became minister for economic warfare and was responsible for British aid to anti-Nazi resistance in occupied Europe, had been outraged by the expulsion of Jewish academics from German universities in the early 1930s, and remained hostile to the Germans throughout and after the war. In the summer of 1942 he wrote to Foreign Secretary Eden, himself no warm admirer of Germany, that 'Germany is, and will remain, even though defeated, the greatest potential danger to our children. It is our primary duty to break her power for evil deeds, now and through the long future.'[10] Dalton's experiences as the minister in charge of the Special Operations Executive (SOE) also led him to the conclusion that no serious resistance to National Socialism could be expected from the Germans.[11]

Within the Labour Party, opinions about the attitude to be adopted towards the German people were divided, but as the war went on, so the negative assessment of the German character came to be more widely accepted. This was illustrated by Labour's relationship with German Social Democrats in exile in London. At first they were welcomed as brother socialists struggling against Hitler. But, after the shocks of the French defeat and the blitz on British cities, memories of earlier collaboration by the SPD in the Kaiser's war effort were revived. By October 1941 the International Secretary of the Labour Party, Frank Gillies, had produced a very hostile memorandum on the foreign policy of the SPD, which soured relations between them and their Labour hosts for the rest of the war. I mention this because if ever there were 'good Germans' in the sense implied by British propaganda at the start of the conflict, then men like Ollenhauer and Vogel, who had been struggling against the Nazis for years and whose comrades, like Kurt Schumacher, were rotting in Nazi concentration camps, should have been prize examples. Some strident voices in the Labour movement stressed that National Socialism was only a symptom of a more deep-seated German disease. At conferences of the Labour Party and the Trades Union Congress, motions that implied distrust and fear of the Germans were discussed and on occasion carried. In September 1942 the leader of the TUC attacked those 'who profess and plead for sympathy for the German people'. He was convinced that until 'the German people, not alone their gangster rulers, have meted out to them what they have meted out to millions of their fellow-creatures ... the German people will again, if not prevented ... make another attempt to enslave Europe.' This statement was endorsed by the historian and Fellow of All Souls, A.L. Rowse, with the comment that 'one had to be either very clever or very silly not to be able to see that something is dangerously wrong with the Germans. Ordinary people ... whose point of view has been expressed by ... [the] President of the TUC... appreciate this perfectly well.'[12] In April 1944, a report by the NEC of the Labour Party to its forthcoming conference, a report largely influenced by Dalton, proposed harsh, although certainly not atrocious, treatment for Germans after the war, and in a section about 'the question of German responsibility', it claimed that the 'large number of decent, kindly Germans' were 'singularly ineffective in restraining the bad Germans'. It pointed to the millions who had participated in atrocities in occupied Europe, and also to the systematic effort made since 1933 'to corrupt and brutalize all German youth'.[13]

I have stressed this attitude amongst Labour politicians because their party had traditionally represented internationalist and even pacifist attitudes, and because they had been members of a socialist international which included the German Social Democrats. The extent to which they accepted a blanket condemnation of the Germans is indicative of a general shift in British attitudes.

However, it would be unwise and unhistorical to draw too many conclusions about the British view of German character during the war, since it always contained an element of the ambivalence that we noted at the beginning. There was a marked reluctance to tar all Germans with the same brush. This can be seen in the reaction to what was probably the most notoriously anti-German piece of propaganda to appear in Britain during the war, Robert Vansittart's *Black Record*, which was published in 1941 and was also broadcast by the BBC. In it Vansittart presented German history as a long series of brutal aggressions. Amongst other dubious claims, he argued that German barbarism had defeated Latin civilization at the battle of Adrianople in the year 378. This assertion provoked a public response from an exiled German social democrat, Heinrich Fraenkel, who drily remarked that it was a 'somewhat inadequate explanation for the fall of the Roman Empire'. His sharp critique of Vansittart was published by the Fabian Society, and many Labour or left-inclined intellectuals, such as Philip Noel-Baker, Julian Huxley, Harold Laski and C.E.M. Joad, resisted the notion of collective guilt being applied to the Germans. The Morgenthau Plan, for example, met much criticism in Labour circles because of its vengeful and impracticable character. It was accepted that the Germans had to be integrated into the community of nations as soon as possible after the war.[14]

Even the hawkish members of the Labour movement agreed that too harsh a policy towards Germans would be unacceptable. In February 1945, Bevin warned against making 60 million people in the centre of Europe a submerged labour force which could bring down the living standards of other countries, and in May he was telling the Labour Party conference that Britain could not leave 60 million Germans derelict, if only because neither the British nor the Americans had the means to feed them.[15] On 8 February 1945, Labour's *Daily Herald* advised its readers that every effort should be made to help develop a genuine German democracy, and in the House of Commons the Labour spokesman Arthur Greenwood pointed out that no nation could benefit from the more or less permanent impoverishment of 60 or 80 million people.[16]

It should be noted, however, that these more humane views towards Germany were not associated with a fundamentally optimistic attitude to the German character. On the British side there was a widespread belief that the behaviour of the Germans since 1933 had been such that it would take years before they could return as full members to the family of nations. Attlee himself told the House of Commons during the debate on the Yalta Conference that the Germans had actively supported their rulers and that 'it was idle to think that the process of converting the Germans from the barbarities into which they have sunk to civilization was not going to take a long time.' The answer to all this lay in the concept that Lothar Kettenacker has dealt with in his important study of wartime planning, namely 're-education', a concept which in itself implied a negative attitude to the German national character.

To appreciate the widespread nature of this attitude, it is instructive to record an independent, moderate voice in British political discourse, that of *The Economist*. Here was a journal whose editors were well aware of the need for a peace which would involve reconciliation between Britain and a German nation whose economic well-being was vital for British prosperity. However, on 6 January 1945, it pointed out that it would be wrong to look on 'Germany as something that has been perverted by a gang of criminals. The totalitarian regime boasts of many gangster types in high positions, but it has been born out of very powerful anti-democratic tendencies. Overwhelming material superiority will in the end defeat its armed forces, but unless it is also defeated politically, it may tend to revive.'[17] Four days later, one of the leading German experts in the British Foreign Office, Con O'Neill, wrote a memorandum on 'German Reactions to Defeat' in which he warned that the Germans might try to work for an alliance with Russia. He described them in the following terms: 'National Socialism has been no more than a special form of organisation of the instincts and capacities of the German people. Other forms of totalitarian organisation almost equally unpleasant and effective may occur, for those instincts and capacities will remain largely what they are.'[18]

When considering British views of the Germans in 1945, it should, I think, be remembered that in the early months of that year the defeat of Germany did not yet seem imminent. The temporary success of Rundstedt's offensive in the west in mid-December 1944 had shaken British confidence. Readers of journals like *The Economist* and the *Spectator* were told that there was a long way to go before the war was over, and, as late as mid-March 1945, the *Spectator* was approvingly quoting the words of Sir James Grigg in the House of Commons to the effect that 'the war is not yet won, no one can say when it will end, and to indulge [in speculation] is not only dangerous to morale, but ... might even postpone what everybody wishes.'[19] So even the educated public did not have much time to reorient itself from warlike modes of thought to the needs of European reconstruction.

By the time Hitler had committed suicide and the Russians had conquered Berlin, satisfaction at the prospect of German surrender had been coloured by another shocking event: the liberation of concentration camps in Germany such as Belsen and Buchenwald. Even among the relatively sophisticated readers of the two above-mentioned journals, it is clear that the horrors of the camps raised all over again the issue of German guilt and of whether there was not something inherently wicked in the German character. I have already mentioned the reaction of one Member of Parliament published in the *Spectator*, but even *The Economist* was moved to remark that 'it would be wrong to hold the German people fully to blame for the horrors of the concentration camps. But it would be even more wrong to hold them wholly blameless. There must be a deep-seated moral sickness in a people that could find enough members to do such dirty work, in a people that, dictatorship or no, could tolerate such things, in a people whose senses were so indelicate that they could now profess ignorance of what for twelve years has been stinking to high heaven in their midst.' The rather daunting conclusion drawn was that 'the German people will have to spend many years on their knees before the stains are scrubbed out.'[20]

'Re-education' was indeed the buzz word of this final phase of military operations against Germany, and some remarkable things were expected of it. O'Neill, in his memorandum of 10 January 1945, gave as his solution for the German problem the suggestion that 'Germany must be encouraged to aim at being a super-Sweden, cleaner, better planned and healthier than any state ever was before.'[21]

The ambivalence of the British on this issue can be illustrated by the reactions to the famous 'non-fraternization' order issued to

British troops by Field Marshal Montgomery in March 1945. This was approvingly noted by the *Spectator*, which argued that the bulk of the German people, who had applauded Hitler's victories, 'would act again precisely as they acted in 1939, 1940 and 1941 if they got the chance. Nothing would encourage them more than any attitude on the part of the Allied troops which suggested that the Allies were ready tolerantly to let byegones be byegones. "Stern Justice" should be the byword for years to come.'[22] *The Economist*, on the other hand, was far less enchanted by the non-fraternization order. It rejected the idea that Montgomery's ban on any social relations with Germans could be continued into the occupation period after the end of hostilities by saying, 'Of all the unrealistic notions that are now current on conditions in post-war Germany, that would be the most fantastic.'[23]

It should also be pointed out that even the harsher critics of the Germans at this time distanced themselves from the racism of the Vansittartist stamp. Most commentators in the early months of 1945 seemed agreed that the Germans could not be trusted for a considerable period – *The Economist* thought this should not exceed five years – during which time they should be faced with harsh conditions and strict Allied controls. But all seemed agreed that somehow the Germans could and should be re-educated into becoming participant members of the European family of nations.

Hence the consensus about the German character that had existed in the First World War, which had reappeared during the Second, did make its mark in the public debate in Britain in the spring of 1945. Re-education meant above all a period of harsh treatment for Germany, coupled with demilitarization and the elimination of nationalist tendencies in education and cultural policy. The harshness was in any case an inevitable part of the post-war situation in Germany, but it was not long before the Anglo-Saxon occupiers, at any rate, realized what intelligent economists had been saying all along, namely that European recovery could not occur without German recovery. On the educational front a great deal was done to eliminate odious examples of racism and xenophobia from German textbooks and teaching materials. But when it came to the practicalities of occupation, the obsession with peculiarities of national character began to wane quite rapidly. In the educational branch of the British

Control Commission this was especially noticeable. In August 1948 its deputy director wrote pointedly to the Foreign Office: 'We detest the word re-education as much as the Germans. This is an Education Branch, not a 'Re-education' Branch, and the word has never been used in our directives.'[24] Before long, therefore, common sense overcame the myths about national character, and for that we can all be thankful.

NOTES

1. Mavis Tate MP, 'More on Buchenwald', *Spectator*, no. 6097, 4 May 1945, pp 402–3.
2. Heinrich von Sybel, 'The German Empire', *Fortnightly Review* (New Series, vol IX, London 1871), pp 1–16.
3. He wrote that this showed a new side of the German character: 'a narrow-minded, proud, intolerant Prussian *chauvinism*. And the worst of it is that he is forming a school.' Quoted by Peter Winzen, 'Treitschke's Influence on the Rise of Imperialist and Anti-British Nationalism in Germany', in P. Kennedy and A.J. Nicholls (eds), *Nationalist and Racialist Movements in Britain and Germany Before 1914* (London, 1981), p 161.
4. See Martin Gilbert, *Sir Horace Rumbold. Portrait of a Diplomat, 1869–1941* (London, 1973), pp 367–86.
5. *Daily Mail*, 10 July 1933, quoted by F.R. Gannon in *The British Press and Germany 1936–1939* (Oxford, 1971), p 33.
6. Gannon, *British Press and Germany*, p 46, quoting from G.E.R. Gedye, 'Impressions of Hitler's Germany', *Contemporary Review*, June 1933.
7. All the above quotations come from Lothar Kettenacker, *Krieg zur Friedenssicherung. Die Deutschlandplanung der britischen Regierung während des zweiten Weltkrieges* (Göttingen, 1989), pp 31–2.
8. Kettenacker, *Krieg zur Friedenssicherung*, p 35.
9. Ibid, p 194 n.7.
10. Quoted in T.D. Burridge, *British Labour and Hitler's War* (London, 1976), p 66.
11. See his diary comments on this subject in May 1944, in Ben Pimlott (ed), *The Second World War Diary of Hugh Dalton* (London, 1986), p 747.
12. Burridge, *British Labour and Hitler's War*, p 65, citing A.L. Rowse in *Tribune*, 11 September 1942.
13. Burridge, *British Labour and Hitler's War*, p 119.
14. For this discussion, see A.J. Nicholls, 'Die britische Linke und der 20. Juli 1944', in K.-J. Müller and D.N. Dilkes (eds), *Großbritannien und der deutsche Widerstand 1933–1944* (Paderborn, 1994), pp 123–36.
15. Alan Bullock, *The Life and Times of Ernest Bevin. Volume II: Minister of Labour 1940–1945*, (London, 1967), pp 382–4.
16. Burridge, *Labour and Hitler's War*, p 154.

17. 'Germany at War', *The Economist*, vol CXLVIII, 6 January 1945.
18. Kettenacker, *Krieg zur Friedenssicherung*, p 534.
19. 'Across the Rhine', *Spectator*, no. 6090, 16 March 1945, p 237.
20. 'Notes of the Week', *The Economist*, 21 April 1945, p 506.
21. See n. 17 above.
22. 'A Spectator's Notebook', *Spectator*, 30 March 1945, no. 6090.
23. 'Notes of the Week', *The Economist*, 31 March 1945, p 408.
24. Cited by Kurt Jürgensen, 'The Concept and Practice of "Re-education" in Germany 1945–50', in N. Pronay and K. Wilson (eds), *The Political Re-education of Germany and Her Allies* (London, 1985), p 84.

3

'A Mixture of Stubborn Resistance and Sudden Surrender': The British Media Report on the End of the War in Europe[1]

ULRIKE JORDAN

On 4 May 1945 the *News Chronicle* carried these headlines:

> The last hours are at hand. Hamburg has fallen: the British and the Russians have linked on the Baltic front. British troops are officially stated to have reached the Kiel Canal. Copenhagen messages say they are across the Danish frontier.[2]

Germany's unconditional surrender was imminent. On the evening of the previous day, 3 May, the BBC 9 o'clock news had begun: 'From Hamburg to Rangoon the tide of victory flows on.'[3] This tide of victory was both well documented and commented on in the British media. From the last days of April, it was immediately apparent to readers and listeners in the British Isles that the war was coming to an end. On 1 May they learnt the details of how VE Day would be celebrated. Within another week the German capitulations were signed and the VE Day celebrations could go ahead.[4]

This chapter will examine the news and media coverage during those crucial days just before and after the end of the war. The end of the war in Europe was reported extensively to the British public, who were accustomed to the BBC's detailed news coverage, most notably through the *War Reports* series. This live coverage from the war theatres had been transmitted every evening after the 9 o'clock evening news. The newspapers, radio broadcasts, newsreels and magazines reflected day-to-day developments, military defeats and victories, in minute detail. Among the important topics covered by the media reportage were Himmler's peace feelers, the advancing and meeting of Allied troops at Torgau, the battle of Berlin, Hitler's death, and the capitulations of the German army and the German government. Instead of focusing on these well-known developments and their media coverage, however, I will concentrate on the broader issues of what might be called *the fabric of image*, that is, the facets of the image of Germany and the Germans put forward in the British media. The sources on which this chapter is based are the two most widely noticed media of the 1940s: newspapers and radio.

I have chosen to concentrate on the most widespread and influential examples within each of these two media: the BBC radio news, most importantly the evening news at 9 o'clock, and the *Daily Mail*, the *Daily Telegraph*, *The Times*, the *News Chronicle*, the *Evening Standard* and the *Morning Star*. The two media had existed in a mutually influential relationship since 1926, when the BBC was created by royal charter, soon becoming what A.J.P. Taylor termed a 'cultural dictatorship', a monopolistic corporation.[5] The BBC from the beginning issued news bulletins on a regular basis, which corresponded to a change that occurred with respect to the profile of newspapers. The morning newspapers began to aspire to a national importance and circulation, a goal that implied earlier printing to ensure nationwide delivery. So radio and newspapers fulfilled different roles in the provision of information. During the Second World War these roles, which had been initially defined in the 1920s, expanded further. Radio had an immediate political impact, bringing the voices of leading statesmen, most importantly the Prime Minister himself, directly to the homes of citizens. In the field of newspapers, political and personal affiliations were crucial, as was the fact that for the first time the masses read a daily newspaper, such as Lord Northcliffe's *Daily Mail* and Lord Beaverbrook's *Daily Express*. An extraordinary case was the *Daily Mirror*, which had no proprietor, functioned as a platform for democratic opinion and reached its maximum circulation during the war. The social and political affiliations of the papers were clearly discernible, ranging from *The Times* at the establishment end of the social scale, to the *Daily Herald*, which was read by trade unionists. An exception to this rule was the

Beaverbrook-owned *Daily Express*, which was read by a cross section of Britain's social and political spectrum. Another facet of publicized opinion, which can only be touched upon here, were the weekly journals, which enjoyed wide popularity and were for many the most important source of background information on current events. These included such well-known publications as the *Spectator*, the *Saturday Review* and the *New Statesman*.[6]

In my analysis of media coverage I shall focus on the period from the announcement of Hitler's death on 1 May to the two separate capitulations of the German army on 4 and 7 May. Whereas the radio news provides news summaries and informative or illustrative reports, newspapers offer information and commentary in a variety of forms, including the leader, features, and letters to the editor. This chapter cannot provide a detailed look at individual newspapers and radio broadcasts. Instead, it will examine a selection of papers and radio news in an attempt to put together a picture of information and commentary on certain questions. It is, of course, true that censorship affected the BBC and the newspapers in different ways, and this fact should be borne in mind at all times.[7] In assembling impressions of the images of Germany and the Germans projected by the British media, we will address three questions.

First, how was the individual and collective mentality of the Germans evaluated? Most importantly in this respect, we will ask how news of the mass murder of the Jews and other Nazi victims in the concentration and death camps was received by the British public and reflected in the media. Another aspect of the German mentality that will be assessed is the relationship between ordinary Germans and Nazi officials, especially Hitler. Second, we shall ask whether the Germans in Britain – prisoners-of-war and refugees – were presented differently from the Germans in Germany. Third, we will ask whether any general assessments of the twelve years of Nazi dictatorship were offered, and if so, what these assessments dwelt upon? Of special interest to historians is the question of continuity: was the period from 1933 to 1945 regarded as a separate entity, or were attempts made to reach wide-ranging conclusions about the German mentality in general.

In examining the central question of how German attitudes towards Nazi policies and the Nazi hierarchy were evaluated by the British media, I shall start with the problem of the death camps and the underlying issue of collective guilt. Events in April and May 1945 had brought the horrible truth home to both Allied and German civilians. On 15 April 1945 British troops liberated Bergen-Belsen. Four days before that, concentration camp inmates had liberated Buchenwald and handed it over to the Americans. Similar actions happened in other camps.[8] The discovery, the shock and the attempt to find initial psychological and moral responses to issues such as knowledge, responsibility and guilt are reflected in a large number of British newspaper articles. In addition, there was huge public interest in the documentary films on Bergen-Belsen, Buchenwald and Dachau that were shown in England.[9] What tendencies can be distinguished in media commentary?

The issue was approached in a variety of ways. Official British reactions based on information provided by eyewitnesses were represented by reports about the parliamentary group visiting the concentration camps. On 26 April, the *Daily Mail*, like many other papers, carried a lengthy statement by Sidney Silverman MP, member of the delegation:

> One of the Parliamentary delegates just back from the Buchenwald horror camp, Mr. S.S. Silverman, Labour M.P. for Nelson and Colne, said in London last night that what he had seen was appalling beyond belief.... Mr. Silverman, who was speaking to the British section of the World Jewish Congress at Toynbee Hall, said that Buchenwald was established in 1933, but the British Foreign Office kept back the truth about the horror camps for six years in the hope of appeasing the Germans. 'I know the facts about Buchenwald,' he said. 'If I had been a German citizen who knew these facts and who knew, too, that a breath, a whisper, of protest would have meant that my own children would have been in Buchenwald the next morning, I would not have had the courage to do anything.' Mr Silverman was reported to say that 'there was a greater blame on those who knew the facts, who could have protested in safety and who did not, than on those who could only protest at the risk of sharing the same fate'.[10]

In the context of reporting the subsequent House of Lords debate on atrocities, Vansittart's proposal of an annual repentance day for Germany was noted in the *Daily Express* of 2 May. Together with the report on a *Daily Express* exhibition entitled 'The Horror

Camps', this confirmed the general line, which was to see the entire German people as guilty.[11] On the same day the *Daily Herald* carried an article entitled 'These Germans Unashamed'. Referring to the parliamentary delegation again, it quoted Lord Stanhope: 'The Germans I saw visiting the camp seemed, I thought, to care very little.'[12] The article also referred to Lord Addison's impression that the German people undeniably knew about the camps.[13] Moving on to the issues of re-education, the article quoted the theory of 'appallingly successful disciplining' of the German mind, as it was put forward during the Lords' debate.[14] Finally, the article reported Lord Simon's denial during the debate that there had been any considerable resistance movement in Germany.[15]

The changing attitudes of professional and academic bodies in Britain are also reflected in the papers. Most noteworthy are comments by the International Student Service and the British trade unions. On 5 May the *Daily Herald* covered the Blackpool conference of the *National Union of Distributive and Allied Workers*.[16] One of the most important outcomes of the discussions was a reversal of the union's position on the treatment of Germany. Previously, the line taken by the union had been that such crimes could not be pinned on the German people. On 4 May, however, a resolution was passed that for Germany and Japan retribution and atonement must follow military defeat. Territorial changes were also considered necessary for future peace and stability in Europe. Moreover, a vote of 76,000-plus to 62,000-plus defeated an amendment which stated that the roots of war and fascism were to be found 'in no single nation but in capitalism'.[17] The International Student Service, which had in 1943 recorded a view that relief workers should go to ex-enemy countries in the spirit of 'sharing a sense of guilt', sent a letter to the editor of the *Daily Telegraph* to disclaim this statement as representative of its current views. This letter, printed on 4 May 1945, was a direct reaction to criticism on that point which had previously been printed in the *Telegraph*.[18]

Against the background of this more or less unanimous opinion in the media, a letter to the editor in the *Daily Mail* of 27 April stands out. Given the headline 'Letter from a British Hitler?' by the paper, the letter read:

> Sir, – Emaciated bodies (in atrocity pictures) are more probably evidence of typhus deaths, the result of Allied destruction of habitations. Now publish some pictures of civilian dead of Le Havre and other places destroyed by soldiery of Jew-blighted United Nations. Your one-sided presentation of horrors of war is un-English, and worthy only of slimy, Jewish owners of your paper. – J.M.C. (Name and address not given)'.[19]

This disturbing piece highlights the important issue of the British fascists' reaction to the end of the war, one not reflected in newspapers and the media.

Another key issue in the process of evaluating individual and collective German mentalities was the relationship between Hitler and the German people. We might ask how this issue was seen in April–May 1945 against the background of German defeat. The *Daily Express* carried an important article about the relationship between the German people and Hitler on 3 May 1945. Under the headline, 'Germans still love that man', Selkin Panton reported from Weimar, commenting on an opinion poll he had taken there. Quite characteristically, parallels are drawn with the end of the First World War. After quoting a young man who claimed that the Germans still really loved Hitler, the author wrote:

> This reply, and others, have convinced me that Hitler still grips the souls of most Germans. They excuse him by saying that he was led astray by the men round him, especially Ribbentrop. This is what the Germans said about the Kaiser after the last war.[20]

References to the 'Hitler myth', after his confirmed death, can be found in both newspapers and radio.[21] The key issue here is the reporting of speculation about his death. The 6 o'clock news of 2 May may stand as an example for many:

> The German story of how Hitler met his death – a hero, fighting to his last breath, in the Chancellery in Berlin – has fallen flat ... opinion in the Allied world seems unanimous that the version of Hitler's fate put out by the German Home Service last night is an invention designed to build up the legend of a heroic Führer for future generations.[22]

The ascribing of collective guilt, and anxiety about the persistence of a Führer cult, seems to dominate the discussion of the German mentality on the air and, especially, in print.

My second main question about the image of Germans in Britain yields rather different, although equally controversial, results. The newspapers discussed at length the living and working conditions of German prisoners-of-war. Under the title 'How Geneva Convention works in the fields of Essex', the *Daily Mail* of 26 April reported on the farm work done by German prisoners-of-war.[23] Open criticism of the level of rations they received – twice that of British civilians – was expressed in both text and photograph. But the burden of feeding the unwelcome German prisoners-of-war was balanced by the prospect of their role during the coming occupation. On 1 May, the *Daily Express* commented on the role of selected German prisoners-of-war:

> Carefully chosen German prisoners-of-war will soon be going back to Germany. They will go with the British Army of occupation and be attached to the Allied Control Commission. The prisoners – soldiers, sailors and airmen, officers and men – will have the job of telling the German people what Britain is like. They have been chosen for their intelligence and comparative friendliness to this country. For months past they have been taken out under escort to see Britain for themselves.[24]

On 9 May, the 6 o'clock news reported the British Government's decision to use German prisoners-of-war in considerable numbers to help in the housing programme in Britain.[25]

The image of the refugee from Nazi Germany was no less ambiguous. Even in 1945, old misgivings about identities and trustworthiness persisted and found their way into the media. On 2 May, the House of Lords debated the position of the roughly 40,000 Germans in Britain. The controversy between Lord Reading and Lord Ailwyn, who refused to believe that the refugees would not hinder ex-servicemen getting jobs after the war, was reported extensively in the *Daily Herald*. It quoted Lord Reading: 'About 90 per cent of these 40,000 Germans are Jews ... and if they had not been in this country they would have been in German concentration camps. They have lost everything – homes, fortunes and families.'[26] The final statement for the government, by Lord Munster, was also quoted: 'There is no complacency.... There is no infiltration into British Government departments, and there is no fear that by remaining in this country the full employment of Service people will be prejudiced.'[27]

The *Daily Express* also reported this controversy on 3 May. It informed its readers that of the 40,000 Germans in Britain, quoting Lord Reading, 'many were over 50, and 10,000 were children. Most were poor. But some have built 450 factories in this country and are employing between 20,000 and 30,000 British workpeople.'[28] The image of Germans in Britain at this time was less coloured by immediate discoveries and news than was the assessment of the Nazi mentality. Practical considerations such as the usefulness of German labour both in Britain and in Germany under the direction of the future Control Commission, as well as a more balanced assessment of the impact of refugees on British society since 1933, produced a considerably more differentiated picture.

Finally, my third question on general assessments raises the larger issues of historical perspective. The whole political spectrum of newspapers looked back at the years from 1920 to 1945. The element of comparison between the end of the First and that of the Second World War comes into play again. As early as 30 April, Guy Ramsey wrote a piece under the title '1920–1945: The Story of a Tyranny' in the *Daily Mail*. He built his argument around notions of the inevitability of Hitler's rise because of the thoroughly mystical nature of the German relationship with government and power:

> For generations, Germany had lived on vicarious glory, but now there was no Kaiser in eagle-helm and medals in Potsdam. In his place sat Cobbler Ebert and a committee of businessmen. Without that focus of their life – a focus for which they had been prepared to kiss the rod that flogged them and lick the boot that kicked them – the Germans were lost.[29]

Ramsay makes the point that underlying features in the German political and psychological condition made Hitler's rise inevitable.[30]

Although most articles concentrate on Hitler, profiles of other elite Nazis also appear. Admiral of the Fleet Karl Dönitz was portrayed in the *Daily Mail* by Guy Ramsey a day after his induction as Hitler's successor. In this racy pen-portrait there is one central reference point: the theme of continuity between the First and Second World Wars.

The background of Dönitz is the background of the whole German Navy ever since the Hohenzollern who last challenged the world gave Germany a fleet ... the soldiers have turned hating eyes on France and dismissed British land forces as, last time, a 'contemptible little army' and, this, as 'an army of amateurs'.[31]

A lengthy character portrait of the 'Organiser of Total Blackout of Truth in Germany', Joseph Goebbels, appeared in the *Daily Telegraph* on 4 May 1945.[32] J.L. Garvin, writing under the headline 'Hitler's Last Testament of Calamity' in the *Daily Telegraph* a day earlier, asked:

> What of others who were chiefs in the criminal camorra of Nazidom? They have to be produced living or truly certified dead. Fat Goering, who piled up wealth and indulged in fantastic ostentation like one of the degenerate Caesars, was a spurious good fellow who could kill with a leer.... What of Ribbentrop? With ineffable vanity and shallowness, he made himself Foreign Minister by ceaselessly insinuating flattery of Hitler, who knew no language but his own and depended much on this pallid sycophant.[33]

This article also refers to a historical continuity leading from Frederick the Great to the First World War and to 1945. Military landmarks of the last days of the Second World War thus acquire symbolic meaning: 'A still more powerful symbol is the linking up of the Western and Russian Armies.... Strangely enough, the meeting began last week at Torgau, in Saxony. There Frederick the Great fought his last great battle.' And Garvin goes on to link 1945 with 1918:

> German militarism was beaten fair and square in the last war. They denied it, because the Allies failed to push victory right home and dictate peace at Berlin. Their drilled and strutting pride from generation to generation – largely based on a false version of their real history and character – could not bear the truth in 1918 and after.... They have been beaten at the second challenge as no people was ever beaten.[34]

On the issue of the capitulation, other attempts were made to connect the end of the First and Second World Wars. On 8 May, the *Daily Telegraph* carried two letters to the editor that dealt with 'German legends and myths of 1945', especially a new version of the stab-in-the-back legend of 1919.[35] In the view of one reader, whose letter is printed in a prominent position next to a general overview of the 'six climacterics' of the war, two most dangerous legends were being entwined:

> The first legend is clearly the 1945 successor of the 1919 'stab in the back' myth, the fairy story of the unbeaten German Army which was let down by the home population.... The second legend which emerges is the ignorance of the officer caste about the concentration camp atrocities. It is the most perfect example of the absolute lack of moral ... courage which characterises all Germans.[36]

The *Daily Mail* of the same day, noted for its pro-German leanings in the early 1930s, carried an article by Lord Vansittart, which, in line with his general argument, commented on the 'greatest storm in the story of mankind'.[37] Vansittart also makes an explicit link between the two world wars: 'We should begin by looking far back – to the memories and the spirits of the Empire's 800,000 dead of the first struggle against the abominable Herrenvolk.... Our first vow to-day should be that we will not fail them twice.' He goes on to criticize the failure of the League of Nations through dissension amongst the Allies.[38]

What conclusions can be drawn from this necessarily impressionistic view of general assessments of the immediately preceding historical period? We may cautiously conclude that certain elements that we have encountered in the context of our first question – the assessment of the German mentality – recur. Militaristic and mystic stereotypes dominate the popular press, whereas the radio news, as in many controversial fields, avoids commentary.

I conclude by looking briefly at reportage of the situation after surrender. Was there a triumphalism on the part of the British, or did the tasks of the imminent occupation period bring a more thoughtful, sober tone? My evidence supports the latter proposition. On 7 May, the *Evening Standard* carried an article by Leslie Randall on a German 'Save us' plea, setting out the admission of helplessness by the Germans who had capitulated to Field Marshal Montgomery.[39] Feeding the millions of starving people was the biggest problem, as Alan Moorehead, writing in the *Daily Express* on the same day, also pointed out in his piece entitled 'Funeral March of Germany'.[40] A few hours after the British public had read these articles, on the afternoon of 8 May 1945, the Prime

Minister, Winston Churchill, announced the end of the war over the wireless from 10 Downing Street.[41] In the months and years ahead, images, commentary and propaganda were to come face to face with the grim realities and compromises of occupation.

NOTES

1. BBC news bulletin, 1 May 1945, 9 p.m., p 12 (quoting Chester Wilmot's description of the opposition on the far bank of the Elbe).
2. *News Chronicle*, 4 May 1945, no. 30,878, p 1.
3. Thursday, 3 May 1945, 9 p.m. BBC news bulletin manuscript, p 1. Copy made available by BBC Kensington House. My sincere thanks for the kind and generous provision of news bulletin manuscripts and copies of newspapers go to Dr Tilmann Remme, BBC Kensington House. For background and further reading, see Asa Briggs, *The War of Words: The History of Broadcasting in the United Kingdom*, vol III (London, 1970); Gerard Mansell, *Let Truth be Told. 50 Years of BBC External Broadcasting* (London, 1982); Anthony Smith, *The British Press since the War* (London 1974); Tom Pocock, *1945: The Dawn Came Up Like Thunder* (London, 1983). For the interwar years, see D.L. LeMahieu, *A Culture for Democracy. Mass Communication and the Cultivated Mind in Britain between the Wars* (Oxford, 1988).
4. Cf. BBC news bulletin, 1 May 1945, 9 p.m., pp 6–7. It was broadcast, for example, that 'First, it's hoped that churches of all denominations will be open for services and prayers and that bells can be rung elsewhere. It's the King's wish that the Sunday after V.E.-Day [sic] should be a day of thanksgiving and prayer.... Even on V.E.-Day [sic] all the street-lamps can't be lit – fuel and light must be saved – but (except round the coast) floodlighting can be turned on ... The Government won't mind you having bonfires – but don't forget salvage. It's hoped that theatres, music halls and cinemas will stay open until their usual time, and that dance halls will stay open later than usual' (ibid, p 6).
5. A.J.P. Taylor, *English History 1914–1945* (Oxford, New York, 1992; 1st edn Oxford, 1965), p 233.
6. Ibid, p 310.
7. See in general, Briggs, *The War of Words*, vol III.
8. See press reports, for example, *Daily Telegraph*, 2 May 1945, no. 28,042, p 3: 'Germans knew all about camps, says Lord Simon'; *Daily Telegraph*, 4 May 1945, no. 28,044, p 5: 'Allied record of Gestapo terrorism'; Cf. also *Daily Mail*, 28 April 1945, on visit by eight MPs and two peers to Buchenwald; cf. also *War Report*, broadcast after the 9 p.m. BBC news bulletin on 1 May 1945, which contained a report by Ian Wilson on the liberation of Dachau.
9. See, for example, the report on the huge interest in the *Daily Express* exhibition of atrocity pictures, 'The Horror Camps', in *Daily Express*, 2 May 1945, no. 14013, p 3. For the interest in films, cf. *Daily Mail*, 28 April 1945: 'The most horrible film ever shown on the screen was exhibited privately in

London yesterday. It is the British Movietone newsreel of atrocities at the German prison camps and will be seen generally in cinemas next week. Nothing has been omitted. The view of those responsible is that the public should be able to see in their entirety the uncensored scenes that no one may in future doubt or ever forget the evidence of German brutality.' Cf. also *Daily Telegraph*, 1 May 1945, on Lord Simon watching the atrocity film. This article also emphasizes that the queues to watch the film stretched from Charing Cross into Trafalgar Square.

For the general background of recent discussions of the topic, there are several good starting points, which can be mentioned only very briefly here. See, for a summary of recent controversies, Thomas Childers and Jane Caplan (eds), *Reevaluating the Third Reich* (New York and London, 1993), especially Ian Kershaw's article on genocide, pp 20–41; cf. also Otto D. Kulka, 'Die deutsche Geschichtsschreibung über den Nationalsozialismus und die "Endlösung": Tendenzen und Entwicklungsphasen 1924–1984', *Historische Zeitschrift*, vol 240 (1985), pp 599–640 for a critical view of the concept of 'historization'. For a general overview of the period 1933–45, see Martin Broszat, *The Hitler State. The Foundation and Development of the Internal Structure of the Third Reich* (London and New York, 1981).

10. *Daily Mail*, 26 April 1945, no. 15280, p 1.
11. *Daily Express*, 2 May 1945, no. 14013, p 3.
12. Ibid.
13. Ibid.
14. Ibid.
15. Ibid. The agreement of HMG (commentary by Lord Simon) to General Eisenhower's action in making the Germans visit Buchenwald concentration camp was followed by another comment by Lord Simon: 'that, though there might have been people in Germany who abominated these methods, no considerable resistance movement sprang up as was the case with the Norwegians, the Dutch and others.'
16. *Daily Herald*, 5 May 1945, no. 9107, p 3.
17. Ibid.
18. *Daily Telegraph*, 4 May 1945, no. 28,044, p 4.
19. *Daily Mail*, 27 April 1945, no. 15,281, p 2. Interesting in the general context of heightened sensibilities *vis-à-vis* fascism in the general public is an article in the *Daily Mirror* of 3 May 1945, p 3. It related the case of an ultimately successful protest by employees at the Medical Supply Association, Gray's Inn Road, London, against the engagement of a former executive member of the British Union of Fascists, Neil Francis-Hawkins.
20. *Daily Express*, 3 May 1945, no. 14013, p 4.
21. Cf. Ian Kershaw, *The 'Hitler Myth'. Image and Reality in the Third Reich* (Oxford, 1987).
22. BBC news bulletin, 2 May 1945, 6 p.m., p 2.
23. *Daily Mail*, 26 April, no. 15,280, p 3.
24. *Daily Express*, 1 May 1945, no. 14,011, p 4.
25. BBC news bulletin, 6 p.m., p 13: 'The Minister of Works said in the Commons today that the prisoners' first job would be to make roads and sewers, get sites ready for building, and so on. If necessary German prisoners

would also be used to clear bombed sites in London.'
26. *Daily Herald*, 3 May 1945, no. 9,107, p 4.
27. Ibid.
28. *Daily Express*, 3 May 1945, no. 14,013, p 2.
29. *Daily Mail*, 30 April, 1945, no. 15,283, p 2.
30. For contemporary newspaper coverage on Hitler, see, for example, in addition to articles mentioned above and below: *Daily Telegraph*, 2 May 1945, no. 28,042, p 4: 'Hitler, blight of many nations'; and *Daily Mail*, 2 May 1945, no. 15,285, p 2: 'This was Adolf Hitler'. The BBC broadcast a special bulletin at 10.20 p.m. on 1 May 1945 on Hitler's death, followed by an additional one at 11.15 p.m. and the midnight news with a profile of Dönitz. For a thoughtful interpretation of the general context, cf. Detlev Peukert, *Inside Nazi Germany* (New Haven, Conn., 1987); Karl Dietrich Bracher, *The Age of Ideologies* (London, 1984); and in general Childers and Caplan (eds), *Reevaluating the Third Reich*.
31. *Daily Mail*, 2 May 1945, no. 15,285, p 2.
32. *Daily Telegraph*, 4 May 1945, no. 28,044, p 4.
33. *Daily Telegraph*, 3 May 1945, no. 28,043, p 4.
35. *Daily Telegraph*, 8 May 1945, no. 28,047, p 4.
36. Ibid.
37. *Daily Mail*, 8 May 1945, no. 15,290, p 2.
38. Ibid.
39. *Evening Standard*, 7 May 1945, no. 37,641, p 3.
40. *Daily Express*, 7 May 1945, no. 14,016, p 1.
41. BBC news bulletin, 8 May 1945, 6 p.m., pp 1–3.

4

Towards Occupation: First Encounters in North Germany

KURT JÜRGENSEN

To start with I should like to qualify the title of this chapter: by the phrase 'towards occupation' I mean the time between 1 May 1945 when the first British soldiers arrived in Schleswig-Holstein, and the beginning of the occupation. The second part of the title covers encounters between the British military forces and the capitulating German forces, the first encounters between the British Military Government detachments and the German civilian authorities, and encounters between the British in Schleswig-Holstein and the German civilian population.

On 4 May 1945, General Admiral von Friedeburg, representative of the German High Command and what may be called the Dönitz government, signed, at the Tactical Headquarters of the 21st Army Group, Lüneberg Heath, the Instrument of Unconditional Surrender of all German armed forces in Holland, in northern Germany including all islands and in Denmark. All hostilities in these areas had to cease at 8.00 a.m. British double summer time on Saturday 5 May 1945. The signing of the unconditional surrender at Field Marshal Montgomery's Tactical Headquarters can be considered as the final encounter on the road towards occupation.[1] I shall refer to this later.

The occupation is not to be understood as an end in itself, but rather as a new experience in British and German history. The occupying power not only had to prevent the revival of a military danger, it also had to rebuild in Germany a community which

53

shared the values of a society that cherished peace and freedom. The task the British had set themselves in theory in the planning stage during the war, and in practice during the period of occupation, may be described as an effort 'to make Germans real Europeans and to make them co-operators in the building up of the new society'.[2] Lord Nathan argued along these lines in May 1942 in a debate launched by Lord Vansittart in the House of Lords.[3] And so, five years later, did Lord Chancellor Viscount Jowitt when broadcasting a message to the German people in June 1947: 'We believe that a happy and contented Germany is a necessary condition of a happy and contented Europe, ... and however distant the goal, it is a goal of which we must not lose sight.'[4]

In those days Robert Birley was in the British Zone as Educational Advisor to the Military Governor. He was fully aware of British responsibilities in Germany. He concluded: 'To rebuild a community, this, in itself, meant that we were committed to an educational task.' His basic idea, that there should be a constant 'stimulus of mind on mind' between the British and the Germans, did not exclude, for him, the idea of re-educating Germany. What was needed? In Birley's view, this was a constant educational effort on both sides.[5]

The year 1945 has to be looked at closely. The month of May, in particular, may be considered as a turning point, after which the British and Germans had to get along with one another. They had a chance to get to know each other, something which many Germans came to appreciate. They were longing for contact with the outside world, from which they had cut themselves off for so long. The initiation of the first contacts was slow, full of scepticism, even distant, but this was soon to change. One of the reasons for this was the British policy of bringing the war to an end as quickly and in as orderly a manner as possible, and of meeting German wishes, provided they did not conflict with British or Allied interests.

I shall now present four encounters. For the first, let us return to Montgomery's Tactical Headquarters on 4 May 1945, at the moment when the Instrument of Surrender was signed in Montgomery's tent. The decisive paragraph reads as follows: 'All

German armed forces in Holland, northern Germany, in Schleswig-Holstein and in Denmark to surrender unconditionally to the Commander-in-Chief 21st Army Group.'[6] After the signing, talks between the British and German sides must have led to Montgomery's secret approval of the official German announcement of this Instrument of Surrender. This announcement differs in three aspects from the English version (which is, however, the authentic text). First, instead of unconditional surrender, the German announcement speaks only of an 'agreed truce between the British and German High Commands'. Second, the phrase in the English version 'the surrender to include all naval ships in the named areas' was revised in the German text to imply that only operations directed against Britain were meant; that is, not those against the Soviet Union. Third, according to the German version, the Instrument of Surrender did not apply to the area between the Bay of Kiel and the German–Danish border.[7] How is all this to be interpreted?

After the signing of the Instrument of Surrender, British troops were ordered not to move forward and certainly not to cross the Kiel Canal. And although this did not include other measures, such as the discreet sending of dispatches in order to bring airfields and war plants under British control, this area was not really occupied until 10 May.[8] How are we to explain the differences between the British text of the Instrument of Surrender and the official German announcement? There is, perhaps, a twofold answer to this. First, Field Marshal Montgomery did not want to impair the authority of Grand Admiral Dönitz and his government, which was located at Flensburg in the non-occupied area. Dönitz's unimpaired authority was required to get the final Instrument of Surrender signed and respected, especially by the German troops still fighting against the Soviets. This was by no means a matter of course, and the full authority of the Dönitz government and of the German High Command was also needed to secure the ceasefire on the eastern front at midnight on 8 May 1945. Orders issued from an occupied area might have been disobeyed, and this would have created a very awkward situation.

Second, Field Marshal Montgomery did seem to understand, for certain reasons, the German will to bring as many soldiers and refugees as possible by ship from the east to the west; that is, from German strongholds in Lithuania and East Prussia to Schleswig-Holstein. Consequently German naval operations were permitted on the Baltic until midnight on 8 May. In the course of the next week, up to 16 May, when the last ship reached a western port, 115,492 German soldiers had, according to German sources, been evacuated by ship.[9] In place of Soviet captivity, they became British prisoners of war, which effectively saved their lives.

For the second encounter, I have to touch on a rather controversial aspect of the immediate post-war period: British relations with the Dönitz government and the German High Command at Flensburg. Even after VE Day the German authorities seem to have retained an astonishing freedom of action. The British paid keen attention to the German announcements broadcast by Dönitz and his associates in the government and High Command. On VE Day, 8 May, *The Times* published an announcement that the German Foreign Minister, Conrad Schwerin von Krosigk, had broadcast from the Flensburg radio transmitter. Its readers may well have been surprised by his vision of a new Germany:

> Justice shall be the supreme law and the main guiding principle. (From inner conviction we must also recognize and respect law as the basis of the relations between the nations).... We may hope that the atmosphere of hatred which today surrounds Germany in the world will give place to a spirit of reconciliation among the nations without which the world cannot recover.[10]

Schwerin von Krosigk solemnly promised that Germany would spare no effort in trying to become once again a worthy member of Christian Western civilization. Three days later, on 11 May, there was another startling broadcast from Flensburg. Field Marshal Busch, Commander-in-Chief, north Germany, sent, as he put it, to all military and civilian authorities the following message:

> By order of the Grand Admiral and in agreement with the British Occupation Authorities, I have taken over command of Schleswig-Holstein and of the areas occupied by the troops of Field Marshal Montgomery.... It is my task to safeguard order and discipline.... All military and civil authorities in my area have been subordinated to me.[11]

This was a quite amazing statement. Could Field Marshal Busch really have been referring to an agreement with the British? Surely he must have misinterpreted what Montgomery had said to him personally on 11 May, the day of his broadcast. For Montgomery and Busch had indeed met at the former's Tactical Headquarters on that very morning.[12] This broadcast created a great stir in England and in other countries, especially the Soviet Union. Mr Roberts of the British Embassy in Moscow reported that the main theme in the Soviet press had been the alleged co-operation of the British government with German military and civilian leaders. He concluded: 'There is no doubt that the Flensburg affair has aroused all the worst suspicions of the Soviet government.'[13] What was the explanation for the Flensburg affair? Mr Vyvyan of the Foreign Office wrote a note to Mr Harvey, Superintending Under-Secretary of State at the F.O. German Department. He may well have been right when he said: 'The incident would appear to be a result of 21st Army Group independent action.'[14] It is certainly true that Montgomery tried to act independently of the Supreme Commander Allied Expeditionary Force wherever possible. He had constant personal contact with Field Marshal Busch through General Kinzel, Busch's liaison officer at Montgomery's headquarters. Above all, he was in personal contact with the Prime Minister, Winston Churchill.

Mr Steel, Foreign Office representative at Supreme Headquarters Allied Expeditionary Force, had admittedly argued: 'It is evident that the German organization in northern Germany is of very little value [to us].'[15] On the other hand Montgomery had his own view and was supported by the Prime Minister. On 14 May, three days after the Busch incident, the Prime Minister rejected Sir Orme Sargent's suggestion that Dönitz and his associates should be dismissed immediately. Churchill argued that Dönitz should be used to force the Germans to accept the terms of surrender. He disregarded the argument that having been in command of German submarines Dönitz was, in the eyes of the British, a war criminal. Churchill raised the question as to whether Dönitz had any power to persuade the Germans to do what the British wanted. He then sent a second letter to Sir Orme Sargent: 'You seem to be startled at Field Marshal Busch giving orders.

The orders seem to be to get the Germans to do exactly what we want them to do. We will never be able to rule Germany apart from the Germans.'[16] But even Churchill could not act against public opinion. Nine days later, the members of the Dönitz government and the German High Command were arrested in a joint action by the Americans, Soviets and British. The puppet government set up by Hitler before he committed suicide had, quite rightly, been brought down. But on a lower level, those German channels of command used by the British remained intact, so that in Schleswig-Holstein it was possible for one million German soldiers to be handled and disbanded by only three British divisions. They were concentrated into two large areas, one on the eastern peninsula of Schleswig-Holstein and one on the western peninsula. From amongst them, so-called German task forces were recruited to do the mine-sweeping and other demolition work. This went on throughout 1945, under British supervision, and it worked quite well.[17]

For my third example I intend to look at the contacts between the British and the German civil authorities. Was there any notion of dealing with a German administration? A great number of papers were produced: by Civil Affairs (G5) at Supreme Headquarters Allied Expeditionary Force until its dissolution in mid-July 1945; by government offices in London and post-surrender committees concerned with Germany; by the Chief of Staff and the Director of Military Government attached to the Commander-in-Chief, 21st Army Group for as long as it continued to exist. In August 1945 the considerably reduced Army Group became the British Army of the Rhine.

So what was the hard core of the ideas disseminated in these papers? I shall look at four main points:

1. Military Government was not supposed to take over the administration in Germany but to establish controls over the German government. The functions of government had to be carried out by German personnel and German administration agencies. I quote from a SHAEF message to the Commander-in-Chief, 21st Army Group, dated 11 May 1945:

It is particularly important that German administrative machinery be established to permit the effective handling of immediate problems at the regional level to include distribution of food, effective utilisation of available transport, and the re-establishment of industrial production to meet military needs and to provide minimum essential civilian requirements in Germany.[18]

It was not intended at this early stage that the British occupation force should *re*-organize the German administration. This meant that the administrative structure of a Prussian province such as Schleswig-Holstein would, for the time being, remain untouched, even though the state of Prussia was considered to be the embodiment of an authoritarian and militaristic spirit. The British were prepared to wait until late October 1945. Only then did the Zone Policy Instruction No. 4 stipulate that the top levels of the administration in Schleswig-Holstein should be amalgamated.[19]

2. Control over the German government had to be exercised by Military Government detachments corresponding to the levels of German government within a region. The members of these detachments were, generally speaking, recruited and trained at Military Government schools in England and in the liberated countries such as Belgium and the Netherlands. I can give an example based on the war diary of the 616 L/R detachment (L = Land; R = Regierungsbezirk). In early 1945 this detachment – for the time being called a unit – was staying at a castle near Antwerp. We can follow the path it took day by day until it was finally placed under the command of the 8 Corps district. The diary entry for 6 May is as follows: 'Orders received from 8 Corps to proceed to Schleswig 12 May, but not to operate until further orders.' On 12 May it reads: 'Reached Schleswig 3 p.m. Took over Regierungspräsident's official residence and arranged offices in Regierungsbezirk's building.'[20] The man in charge of the deployment of the Military Government detachments was Major General Templer, Director of Military Government at the 21st Army Group Headquarters.

3. This was the very moment of the first contacts between the British and the Germans as far as administration was concerned. Let us look at Schleswig as an example. An advance group of the

616 L/R detachment must have visited the building and occupied the offices before, two days later, on 14 May 1945, the detachment Commander summoned the Vice-President to see him. I quote again from the war diary: 'Our intentions were conveyed to him and his cooperation demanded. Officers began to interview the various officials in connection with their functional duties.' The British may well have observed Directive No. 1, 'Germany in the post-surrender period': 'The attitude to the German population of all forces and agencies under your command or control should be just, but firm and distant.'[21] Fraternization was strictly forbidden. The Germans were instructed accordingly by Montgomery's message to the German people.

Let us now look at Schleswig in a broader context. The Commander of the Provincial Detachment in Schleswig-Holstein, Brigadier-General Patrick Henderson, and the Commander of the 21 Kreis Detachment in the same province acted in exactly the same way. They placed themselves under the command of Lieutentant-General Sir Evelyn Barker, Commander of 8 Corps District (HQ at Plön). The Military Government detachments were composed of functional officers who received their instructions, directly or indirectly (following the chain of command), from the Central Executive Officers' Main Headquarters, Military Government, British Zone (Advanced HQ in Berlin/Provincial Detachment – 70 officers – in Kiel).

4. All the detachments of Military Government were reminded of the Supreme Headquarters Directive of 9 November 1944, of which the stated purpose was 'to remove all Nazi and militarist influences from public offices and from the cultural and economic life of the German people'.[22] The denazification of the German administration in 1945 was the responsibility of the Field Security Sections, in conjunction with Military Government detachments. All the mandatory removal categories and the automatic arrest categories were set out in the Handbook of Military Government in Germany. So how did it work in practice? At a meeting in Kiel attended by all detachments and Field Security sections on 6 July 1945, it was recorded: 'Field Security Sections present were aware of the necessity for consulting Military Government *before* the arrest of any public official.'[23] What was the significance of this?

Certainly, policy had to be co-ordinated. It could also mean that Military Government was prepared to compromise when other factors had to be taken into consideration, for instance the efficiency of the administration. As an example, let us look at the situation in Kiel on 14 May 1945. The 312 Provincial Detachment, under Colonel (soon Brigadier) G.P. Henderson's command, had just settled down when some officers were sent to the seat of the Oberpräsidium. The building had been closed for some time. Questionnaires were sent out to the civil servants who had been working there. Once they had been filled in, they were collected and taken to Henderson's office. Henderson made a quick decision. He sent for Dr Otto Hoevermann, the Regierungsdirektor, and made him Oberpräsident of Schleswig-Holstein. Hoevermann was surprised. His spontaneous reaction was to draw Henderson's attention to the fact, mentioned in the questionnaire, that he had been a party member since 1937 and that he had held a modest command position within the party as a 'Blockleiter'. Henderson seemed to be embarrassed, but only for a short while. Then he said: 'Our way of acting is not dogmatic but pragmatic. The man on the ground has to decide. You know the job you have to do. The efficiency of administration has priority.' This was no exception. The administration of the Regional Food Office, for example, evolved along much the same lines.[24]

Later on, Hoevermann's appointment was greatly criticized. Mr Steel, Chief of the Political Division, was in general agreement regarding the desirability of excluding 'neo-Nazis' from important positions in the administration. Hoevermann's record showed that he was unsuitable for rebuilding a democratic Germany. Major General Balfour, Chief of the Internal Affairs and Communications Division, wrote to Military Government, 8 Corps District, on 23 September 1945: 'I do not press for Hoevermann's immediate dismissal but I request that every effort be made to find a suitable replacement for him with the least delay.'[25] On 15 November Dr Hoevermann was replaced by a well-known member of the German Resistance movement who had survived a death sentence, Theodor Steltzer.

Denazification was much more strict in the educational and academic field. After the surrender, schools and universities had to be closed, but by June 1945 Donald Riddy, Director of

Education Branch, was already arguing as follows: 'The intellectual life of Germany is unlikely to recover from the disastrous corruption of Nazism or redevelop towards usefulness in the civilised world until its academic institutions resume activity.'[26] The reopening of Kiel University in a former armaments factory, since its own premises had been completely destroyed, is a story in itself. It is a story full of encounters between the British and the Germans. Incidentally, Dr Hoevermann was very eager to have the university reopened. His British interlocutor was Mr Wilcox, Education Officer, who helped to get the building released from British Property Control and who managed to organize help from the army to get the factory building cleared of equipment and rubble. The university was reopened on 27 November 1945 by the Provincial Detachment Commander, Brigadier G.P. Henderson, and Oberpräsident Theodor Steltzer. Their speeches were similar in tone: the university was to be devoted to the sciences, whose practitioners were aware of their social responsibility. The university was to serve the truth and, by so doing, help to build bridges between defeated Germany on the one hand, which was on the path towards regeneration, and the victorious countries on the other.[27]

Lack of space makes it necessary to summarize my fourth example of Anglo-German encounters, which may be considered as the most important: more or less formal and informal contacts between the British and the Germans at lower levels. Certainly, at the beginning of the occupation the British were instructed to comply with Directive No. 1, paragraph 8:

> You will strongly discourage fraternisation between Allied forces and the German population. In particular, you will reduce to a minimum all contact between forces under your command and German forces not yet demobilised. In general, contact with German officials should be as little as is necessary in order to ensure the adequate supervision of administration.[28]

In the early stages, life under occupation meant that people had to be fed, housed and kept well informed about British orders and measures. People also had to be confronted with the horrors of the concentration camps so that they would understand how corrupt the Nazi regime was. To take Flensburg as an example: the last issue of the German local newspaper is dated 9 May 1945. The British Press Officer, Sergeant Frank Alexander, appeared on 10 May, and on the following day, under his command, the German technical staff produced the first issue of the *Military Government Journal*. This British press officer was fluent in German, having been born in Berlin to Jewish parents who had emigrated to England a couple of years before the outbreak of war. Sergeant Frank Alexander (who, incidentally, readopted his original name later on and now lives as Professor of History, Ulrich Eyck, in Calgary, Canada) was able to recruit an editorial staff, thanks, in part, to the early discharge of soldiers with editorial qualifications from the concentration areas.[29]

People could apply for jobs to work with the Military Government departments and also with the Army Welfare Service, in lowly capacities, such as service staff. This was a good way of earning some extra food. There were also other forms of employment. In Schleswig-Holstein, 71 units composed of discharged German soldiers worked under British command cutting wood and peat, securing transportation, and assisting the so-called 'Influx Collecting Posts'. People who had crossed the zonal border between the Soviet and British zones had to be directed to special camps for registration and interviewing. Captain Currey, commander in a local area near Lübeck, had to cope with displaced persons who, in 1945, were living in a camp at Plensök. To improve their living conditions, some of the DPs had assaulted and even killed reluctant farmers. Captain Currey formed a mixed British-German police force to secure the area under his command. Other local commanders acted in the same way.[30]

Accommodation had to be handed over to the British, mostly through German channels. I myself had my first contact with an Englishman at Flensburg as a boy, when my parents' home was occupied by a sergeant and his staff. My father tried out his English on him and the Englishman was so pleased that my father was installed as caretaker when this sergeant was absent, and also later on when the house was vacant, after this man had left and another was due to come.

The British were in evidence in the streets. There were parades on special days, such as George VI's birthday on 14 June 1945 and VJ Day on 15 August. Military police controlled the streets during the curfew hours (in June 1945, 10 p.m. to 5 a.m.). Offenders were either warned or arrested for the night or even, in the case of persistent offenders, sent to military courts. Later in the year salvage work and the work of relief groups (belonging to the Council of British Societies for Relief Abroad) generated many good contacts. The Education Branch, co-operating with relief groups, organized school relief meals.

At Christmas 1945, over one hundred children were invited by the Army Welfare Service in Kiel and were treated very generously. Donald Riddy, Head of Education Branch, stressed the importance of showing the German people the benevolent attitude of the occupying power and encouraging a belief in Germany's future.

The first encounters in northern Germany between the British and the Germans showed a two-sided occupation policy. One side was strict control, the firm will to eradicate Nazism and militarism. This included confronting the German population with the atrocities committed by the Nazis, for example in the concentration camp at Bergen-Belsen. The other side was the educational commitment, the firm will to rebuild a healthy and democratic community. When the Chiefs of the Provinces and Länder met at Detmold on 19 November 1945, Major General Templer said in his address to the Germans present at the conference: 'It is the policy of the Commander-in-Chief [Field Marshal Montgomery] to stimulate throughout the population the greatest possible interest in public affairs. We wish to try and teach you to understand democracy as we understand it.'[31] Did this mean, as Wolfgang Rudzio has asked in one of his publications, that British democracy had to be exported to Germany?[32] I do not think so. My view is that what Major General Templer said in his speech is very revealing. He did not mean that British institutions could, or should, be transplanted to German soil. What he did mean, however, is that the Germans should appreciate the values of democracy and freedom in the same way as the British did.

Consequently the 'battle for the German mind' was engaged.

This is the expression which General Sir Brian Robertson used in his final report in June 1950, after five years of service in Germany as Military Governor and British High Commissioner. In 1951 his successor, Sir Ivone Kirkpatrick, used the same expression: 'The battle for the German mind is still in full swing.' I think it is true to say that this battle was also won.[33] Germany has become a democratic state and a respected member of the European family. The battle for the German mind has been won, not *against* Germany but, on the contrary, with the co-operation of the Germans themselves. Thus the British and Allied military victory of 1945 is complete.

NOTES

1. Reimer Hansen, *Das Ende des Dritten Reiches. Die deutsche Kapitulation* (Stuttgart, 1966).
2. Robert Birley, *The German Problem and the Responsibility of Britain*, The Burge Memorial Lecture (SCM Press, London, 3 December 1947).
3. House of Lords, *Parliamentary Debates*, 21 May 1942, pp 1151–2.
4. *British Zone Review. A Montly Review of the Activities of the Control Commission for Germany (B.E.)*, vol 2, no. 1 (28 June 1947), p 20.
5. Birley, *The German Problem and the Responsibility of Britain*.
6. Walter Lüdde-Neurath, *Regierung Dönitz. Die letzten Tage des Dritten Reiches* (Göttingen, 1964), pp 139–40.
7. Erich Murawski, *Der deutsche Wehrmachtbericht 1939–1945* (Boppard/Rhein, 1962), pp 598–9.
8. PRO, WO 171/3854.
9. Militärarchiv – Bundesarchiv Freiburg i.B., RW 44/I 55.
10. *The Times*, 8 May 1945.
11. Militärarchiv – Bundesarchiv Freiburg i.B., RW 44/I 55.
12. PRO, WO 171/3854.
13. PRO, FO 371/46731.
14. Ibid.
15. PRO, FO 371/46785.
16. PRO, FO 371/46914.
17. Kurt Jürgensen, 'Das Ende des Zweiten Weltkriegs in Schleswig-Holstein', *Zeitschrift der Gesellschaft für Schleswig-Holsteinische Geschichte* 120 (1995), pp 147–72.
18. PRO, WO 20575 G.
19. PRO, FO 1006/102 A.
20. PRO, WO 171/8033.
21. Ibid.
22. PRO, WO 205/424.

23. PRO, WO 205/391.
24. Kurt Jürgensen, 'Otto Hoevermann', in *Schleswig-Holsteinisches Biographisches Lexikon*, vol 2 (1971), pp 176–80. This article refers to Hoevermann's private papers.
25. PRO, WO 171/8685.
26. Kurt Jürgensen, *Die Wiedereröffnung der Christian-Albrechts-Universität zu Kiel*, Christiana Albertina 33 (Kiel, 1991). This publication refers to Riddy's private papers.
27. Ibid.
28. PRO, WO 200/215.
29. *Flensburger Tageblatt*, Special Issue, 8 May 1945.
30. Kurt Jürgensen, *Die Briten in Schleswig-Holstein 1945–1949 – Mit Photographien von Gerhard Garms* (Neumünster, 1989) (reference also for the following passages).
31. *Akten zur Vorgeschichte der Bundesrepublik Deutschland 1945–1949*, vol 1 (Munich, 1976), Doc. 5, pp 151–2.
32. Wolfgang Rudzio, 'Export englischer Demokratie? Zur Konzeption der britischen Besatzungspolitik in Deutschland', *Vierteljahrshefte für Zeitgeschichte* 17 (1969), pp 219–22.
33. Quoted from Kurt Jürgensen, 'The Concept and Practice of 'Re-Education' in Germany 1945–1950', in Nicholas Pronay and Keith Wilson (eds), *Political Re-education of Germany and Her Allies after World War II* (London, 1985), pp 83–96.

Part II

5

Fifty Years On: Accounts by Eyewitnesses

The eyewitnesses whose accounts are assembled in this chapter have in common that they all experienced the end of the Second World War in uniform. They also share a lifelong interest in the further political and intellectual development of their respective countries. Lord Annan was a member of the Political Division of the Control Commission for Germany (British Element) from 1945 to 1946. Count Otto von Lambsdorff, a liberal politician of long standing, was a young German soldier at the end of the war, having voluntarily joined the Wehrmacht. He experienced the chaotic circumstances of the post-surrender period while recovering from life-threatening injuries and struggling to re-establish contact with his family. He crossed Allied lines in the early days after surrender, thus sharing the German experience of exposure to rapid military, administrative and political change in April and May 1945.

Peter von Zahn, one of the best-known journalists of post-war Germany ('Reporter der Windrose' and other broadcasts have made him a household name for generations in Germany), describes the British occupation of Germany from the perspective of a critical reporter who was soon working for the newly established North-West German Radio in Hamburg. At another level, however, his experiences resemble those of a multitude of contemporaries in that he did not claim to be a resistance fighter during the Nazi dictatorship. These three accounts can be read as complementary in the sense that they reflect on different aspects of experience, yet all concentrate on north-west Germany. The authors originally delivered these accounts as speeches and an attempt has been made to preserve their spontaneous character.

LORD ANNAN[1]

The end of the war brought terrible days to Germany. They were days of shame. Shame as Belsen was discovered and the story of the Holocaust unfolded. The sense of shame still lives on and I have noted how admirable, how sensitive, German governments have been towards refugees and above all towards Israel. That sense of shame was the root of the *Historikerstreit*. It surfaces in odd ways. In 1993 the elderly Gräfin von der Schulenburg had to obtain for some official purpose registration of her husband's death. She found that the word 'hingerichtet' (executed) had been replaced by the word 'gestorben' (died).

They were also, we may think today, days of shame for the British. No one should blame Churchill for ordering the bombing of Germany. It was the only way the British could retaliate after their defeat in France in 1940. But it became clear to us in the Intelligence Staff of the War Cabinet that night bombing was so inaccurate that German industry was not much damaged. Air Marshal Harris therefore argued that terror bombing of the civilian population could win the war, and Churchill went along with this policy. Was it not by the destruction of Guernica and Rotterdam that the Luftwaffe had triumphed, and who in Britain could forget the destruction in London, Coventry or a dozen other cities? So the terror bombing began with the destruction of Hamburg. It ended with the destruction of Dresden. The messages of the German armed forces which the British cryptographers deciphered, showed that the Soviet armies in the south were striking towards Leipzig not Dresden. But Harris disregarded this evidence and ignored the protest Churchill later made. Mephisto had Faust in his grasp. Nevertheless the Nazi crimes were so stupendous – and the bombardment of London by flying bombs and rockets so recent – that the initial British policy towards Germany in 1945 was harsh. The British felt that no country had done more – indeed at Munich in 1938 had done too much – to help right the wrongs of the Versailles Treaty. In the 1920s the young and the intellectuals, no less than the war veterans, were drawn to Germany. The young admired the famous athlete Dr Pelzer; the intellectuals, Ufa films, the Bauhaus, Brecht–Weill. And what was the result? Hitler. So the occupation began with the farce of non-fraternization. The official policy of the British government was to carry out the Potsdam Agreement of denazification and the dismantling of factories to pay reparations to the Russians.

But this policy in effect meant that Britain would pay reparations to Germany if the German population were to be kept alive. America had imposed hard terms for a loan to Britain and a large part of that loan had to be spent buying food for Germans and financing the costs of the occupation. By 1947, the British Government was forced to ration bread in Britain. That had never happened throughout the war.

The indignation of the British people, who considered they had won the war, can be imagined. German historians usually argue that British policy during the occupation was governed by self-interest. That is true. But British policy was also humanitarian. The great economist Keynes, who was in the Treasury during the war, had ridiculed the policy of revenge and reparations in his polemic against the Versailles Treaty. The British Treasury opposed the Morgenthau Plan or any variation of it.

Meanwhile a second policy had emerged. That was the policy of Military Government. Military Government was faced with a country where millions of displaced persons, including Germans, were on the move. Three out of four houses in the cities were destroyed, seven out of eight damaged. Every major road in Germany was an interminable *Umleitung*. The two great canals were blocked; the few trains crept over improvised bridges.

When P.J. Grigg, Secretary of State for War, saw the man whom Montgomery appointed to be the Military Governor of the British Zone, he told him he must resign himself to the fact that two million people would die of starvation in Europe after the war. General Sir Gerald Templer had no intention of resigning himself to any such calamity. He was a ruthless, incisive, dynamic commander. His smile was ferocious, like a wolf. He first had to feed the Dutch, who were on the verge of starvation. Then he got medicine and food to the concentration camps. Helping two-and-a-half million displaced persons was his next concern. By June 1946, 1.8 million had been repatriated. Meanwhile he put to work half-a-million German prisoners-of-war and women to get in the harvest. When that was achieved, he got German staff officers in the prisoner-of-war camps to identify former miners and recruit others to raise coal production – despite protests from the Russians that he was keeping the German army in being.

Military Government worked on an assumption that appears grotesque today. The assumption was that the occupation of Germany would last for 20 years. Political activities were to develop at the most leisurely pace. First there would be elections in the *Kreise*, then, after an interval, elections in the *Länder*. National parties campaigning in a nation-wide election were a shadow on the horizon. Until then Germany was to be treated as a colony and be re-educated. The model was unquestionably colonial. In fact some of the more senior civilian officers were former British colonial servants. One of them, a redoubtable character called Ingrams, had served in the Middle East and treated Germans as if they were a specially intelligent tribe of Bedouins. As Herr Schumacher once said to me bitterly: 'Wir sind kein Negervolk' (We are no African tribe).

The civilian administrators in the Control Commission were a mixed lot, some out for personal gain, others inspired by high ideals. High among those ideals was the notion that the British would re-educate the German people. Indeed one zealous lady once asked me if I could use my influence to get all performances of Wagner banned as his music inculcated the *Führerprinzip* (leader principle). There was, however, one British official who did not believe in re-education. He put his trust in education. This was Robert Birley. He organized the most successful British innovations: the exchange of visits between British and German teachers, the provision of British libraries, and youth and adult education centres (*Die Brücke*, as these enterprises were called). Most imaginative of all was the Wilton Park Centre run by Heinz Koeppler, where selected German prisoners-of-war who were to rebuild their country went. They were amazed that propaganda played no part in the course. From these beginnings came the annual Königswinter conferences run by the redoubtable Frau Lilo Milchsach. To this day the British have more links of this kind with Germany than they have with any other country, thanks in part to the Deutsch–Englische Gesellschaft.

Military Government's attempt to impose the British pattern of local government was less successful. However, the British could chalk up three successes. The transformation of the German police and the restoration of an independent judiciary was one. The second was the creation of an independent newspaper and broadcasting system (*Die Zeit* and *Nordwestdeutscher Rundfunk*). Journalists were encouraged to be critical even of Military Government, much to the irritation of the Americans. The third was the emergence of a responsible trade union movement. The British told Hans Böckler on no account to follow British practice and allow a multitude of craft unions to form. Instead Böckler formed a number of large trade unions and won rights to representation on the boards of companies.

Many of those in Military Government believed that they were free to govern unimpeded a captive people. But they were to learn that there were institutions that may have no power but have considerable influence. When the towering figure of that great prince of the Church, Cardinal Bishop von Galen of Münster, called on General Templer to protest against the lack of food for his people, he was received by a group of senior officers. The Brigadier in charge of religious affairs, who was a Roman Catholic, dropped on his knee to kiss the Episcopal ring. General Bishop, Templer's Chief of Staff, who was standing next to me, asked anxiously, 'I say, is that fellow on our side or on theirs?'

Military Government was also to learn that there was another activity that would question its policies. It is called politics. Very soon the Foreign Office began to transmit questions that were troubling Members of Parliament. What were these Antifa groups that had formed and offered to identify Nazis? Why was Military Government employing former Nazis in the administration? Why did Military Government never appoint old members of the SPD and appoint only authoritarians?

The Labour government, with Bevin as Foreign Secretary, had an enormous majority in Parliament, but among that majority were 90 or so left-wing socialists who supported the policies of the Soviet Union and accused Bevin of undermining the Potsdam Agreements. And so there emerged within the Control Commission the beginnings of a third policy towards Germany. I had been told not only to report on political developments in the British Zone but to encourage and help political parties to form. It seemed to me that on a multitude of problems, from denazification to the economic recovery, the vast Control Commission bureaucracy was well-meaning but inefficient. Far better to hold elections as soon as possible and turn over the business of governing Germany to the Germans, who showed no signs, then or ever after, of resurrecting totalitarian government. In my many tours of the British Zone, I kept telling Military Government that one or other of the political parties would one day be ruling in our zone, and that we must encourage them if we were to win their hearts, or at least their respect. But Military Government regarded political parties as troublesome bodies. The British were the last of the four powers to approve the establishment of political parties.

Yet as early as the autumn of 1945, Military Government was to be taught the lesson that German politicians were an important force. This was the dismissal of Dr Adenauer as *Oberbürgermeister* (Lord Mayor) of Cologne and the decision to place him under house arrest and forbid him to take part in politics. I interceded on his behalf and my chief agreed that, while he could not be reinstated as *Oberbürgermeister*, the other restrictions on his activities should be lifted; and I had the task of persuading him that the British in fact wished him well. I was never able to dispel Adenauer's suspicion that the Labour Government had ordered his dismissal to help their natural allies, the SPD. For this there was not a shred of evidence.

But it is true that the development of the SPD took up more of my time than the CDU. For this there were two reasons. The first was that the Labour Party activists were justified in thinking that among the *Oberbürgermeisters* and in the nominated councils that the British had appointed, the SPD was under-represented. In Hamburg, the greatly respected Rudolf Petersen presided over a council nominated by the British composed largely from the middle class. Yet when elections came the SPD won a clear victory. The second reason was that the SPD was our bulwark against the

Communists. It was vital for British interests that the SPD, and not the KPD, should become the main left-wing party; but their cadres were old and ill-organized compared with the cells of the KPD. The crisis came when the Soviet Union realized at the end of 1945 that the KPD in their zone would never gain power in free elections. They therefore began a campaign forcibly to amalgamate the SPD and the KPD. There was nothing the Western allies could do to stop the formation of the SED (Socialist Unionist Party) in the Russian sector of Berlin or, of course, in the Soviet Zone. But the younger members of the SPD in the western sectors decided to challenge the bosses of the Central Committee led by Otto Grotewohl.

I spent most of the first three months of 1946 urging my Foreign Office chiefs to support them. They and General Clay were reluctant to intervene. But the younger members of the American political division were also determined to act. I persuaded Schumacher to fly to Berlin, and the Americans organized a press campaign. Germans were forbidden to write anything that could be construed as critical of the policy of any of the occupying powers so I wrote articles for the Berlin press denouncing the Communist leader Walter Ulbricht, a venomous enemy of Britain, for publishing in Sweden in 1940 an article praising the Nazi–Soviet Pact. The Soviets plastered Berlin with posters. We retaliated. The vote on 31 March was overwhelmingly against fusion of the two parties. I have never forgotten the courage of the SPD delegates who risked kidnapping by the Russians or exile like Walther Dahrendorf (father of Ralf), who came to Hamburg.

My last act as a member of the Control Commission was to bring Konrad Adenauer and Kurt Schumacher to Berlin so that they could be told before the news was released to the press that the British were going to form four *Länder* and in effect abandon four-power government of Germany. To Schumacher the divison of Germany was a bitter blow to his electoral hopes. To Adenauer it was what he had always forecast would happen. And so it came about that of the three policies the British operated in 1945 it was the third policy that was to be adopted. It was adopted not by reason but by *force majeure*. In 1947 the British were unable to finance the running of their zone, and the bizone with America was established. With the reform of the currency and the defeat of the Soviet blockade of Berlin, the days of shame were replaced by days of hope.

Were they days of hope for the British? Yes, the British too had hopes of building in Britain a juster society that cared for the poor and was to be less stratified by class distinctions. But they were also days of illusion for the British. Even after their inability to finance the running of their zone in West Germany they still could not adjust to the realities of power. And yet the leadership of Europe was theirs for the asking. The Labour government flung it aside by refusing to join the Schuman Plan.

Conservative governments were worse even than the Labour government. In February 1995 I visited once again Dr Adenauer's house and was shown the menu of the banquet he attended in London in 1952, at which he sat next to Churchill. On the menu Churchill had drawn a diagram of the politics of the Western world. There were three circles: the United States, Europe and the British Commonwealth. The British Commonwealth was even then a political expression, not a political and economic entity that could exert power. Churchill, though only a year or so older than Adenauer, was exhausted, living in the past. His successors, Eden and Butler, had no such excuse and Britain refused to sign the Treaty of Rome. Adenauer understood that the future hung on reconciliation with the French, which ever since 1918 he had tried to achieve. So the leadership of Europe passed into the hands of Adenauer and de Gaulle. They gave their countries self-confidence and pride and were ill-disposed and hostile to mine. As a historian I permit myself an observation. Sadly enough the humiliation of defeat teaches men better than the vanity of victory how to resurrect and inspire their own country.

OTTO GRAF LAMBSDORFF

I will attempt to share with you my memories of the end of the Second World War. At home, I have in fact avoided becoming too involved in this discussion and have perhaps been too reticent. However, it was easy to predict what was going to happen. Indeed, it became a compulsory exercise to have to respond to questions about how one felt on the day Germany surrendered.

On the one hand, there are those who avoid giving a straight answer; and on the other, those who claim to be experts on the matter. But how can anyone know today how they felt at the time, when they were not even ten years old in 1945? I do not object to everything that is said on this subject, but I do take a critical view of much of it.

On 31 March 1945 I was in Thuringia in the heart of Germany as a member of an armoured reconnaissance corps and was seriously wounded in an attack by American low-flying aircraft. I was eighteen years old. On 4 and 8 May 1945, I found myself in a military hospital for prisoners-of-war. The doctors were fighting to save my life. We were completely cut off from the outside world. We had no radios and no newspapers. We naturally did hear about Hitler's death, about the German surrender and about the fact that the war was over. But, given the condition I was in at the time, I can no longer remember how I felt when I heard this news. It was not until later that it sunk in and I understood the nature of the situation facing Germany and also myself. Let me illustrate how I perceived the situation then. In July 1945, the Americans withdrew from Thuringia, under the terms of the Yalta Agreements, and Russian troops appeared overnight. The doctors asked me whether I wanted to remain in Thuringia or accept the Americans' offer of being taken to Hesse.

I said I wanted to stay in Thuringia because I assumed that my mother and my younger brothers and sisters were in East Germany. I was completely unaware of the huge waves of refugees from the East, the 'trecks' as they were called then. It was only because the doctors told me that I would have to undergo two further operations that I went with the Americans to Hesse in the US-occupied zone. It later turned out that my relatives had been part of the great migration westwards. It was their intention to escape the Red Army and reach safe territory. In fact, they reached the safety of the British-occupied zone in Schleswig-Holstein.

Strange as it may seem, a lot of Germans, when they saw British troops, felt that their lives were no longer in danger. Many Germans, therefore, did not view the British as the enemy, as such. I personally came across British soldiers for the first time in

December 1945 when, after being released from captivity, I joined my parents in Schleswig-Holstein. There was no direct contact with the British. There would therefore have been no opportunity for me to engage in 'fraternization'. I was familiar with the ban on fraternization from my time as a prisoner of the Americans. The ban had been imposed by General Eisenhower as well as by Field Marshal Montgomery.

The American soldiers who were our guards did not take it particularly seriously, especially since I sometimes acted as interpreter for them. I do not know for how long the ban was in force. I do, however, recall that British officers began to have occasional social contact with landowners in Westphalia. That was in the summer of 1946.

What were the first measures taken by the occupation authorities? They put in place an administrative system which functioned reasonably well, and they made use of German assistance to do so. This was necessary and was accepted as such. Of course, a degree of arbitrariness was involved. An occupying power has, after all, not been democratically elected. Some of the decisions made were also rather bizarre, such as the Lord Mayor of Cologne, Konrad Adenauer, being sacked for incompetence.

The British occupation authorities went about two things with particular zeal: one was land reform and the other was the dismantling of industry. The land reform was not a success. The dismantling programme, moreover, undermined the competitiveness of British industry, as became clear in the early and mid-1950s. Having been reconstructed from scratch, Germany's industry was more up-to-date and more competitive than that of our European neighbours. The issue of coal mining, however, was a source of great vexation. The Germans were suffering from the bitter cold. Yet the coal mined in the Ruhr was being transported in vast quantities to France, Belgium and Holland. The lorries carrying brown coal briquettes would drive through Cologne and every time they stopped they would be relieved of some of their load by passers-by. But the Archbishop of Cologne, Cardinal Frings, gave a sermon in which he defended the thieves. Indeed, his name was subsequently used to coin a new local expression: to 'frings' coal.

The British influence could be felt very strongly in the media, and in radio in particular. In the summer of 1945, I did not even consider the political situation in general terms. One thing, however, soon became apparent. The British and American Zones contrasted favourably with the Soviet Zone, given what was going on there. Life was also better than in the French Zone. In fact it soon became clear that the way in which the French and Soviet Zones were being run was a reflection of how these countries had experienced the war. They had, after all, been occupied by German troops and, in the case of the Soviet Union in particular, had suffered devastation in the course of the German retreat. By 1946, and particularly after the speech Winston Churchill gave in Zurich, the majority of Germans were aware of the impending conflict between the liberal democracies and the communist dictatorship, given the general political climate. The fact that Germany made a clear decision in favour of freedom and democracy can be considered a historic achievement of Konrad Adenauer and his political friends and supporters.

The general political climate – the conflict between East and West – was undoubtedly one of the most important factors in the political and economic development of Germany after 1945. This went much further than either the Germans or the British could have imagined, from the Morgenthau Plan to the Marshall Plan, from the idea of complete demilitarization to the creation of the Bundeswehr and NATO, to membership of the European Union and the United Nations. I, for one, could never have seen this far ahead in 1945. Whatever progress we have made as a result of international political developments and our own efforts, what seems to me to be more important is whether Germany and the Germans themselves have learnt anything from the horrors of the Nazi past. Let me therefore return once more to 4 and 8 May 1945.

The Second World War came to a close. Hitler's Third Reich ended catastrophically. During the last few months of the war, the country was devastated. Dresden was bombed to rubble for no valid military reason in February. The Germans suffered and grieved. Their cities were razed to the ground; of 10 million refugees who took to the road to escape the revenge of the advancing Soviet Army, hundreds of thousands died from cold, hunger and sheer exhaustion; the survivors arrived in a wasteland of death and destruction. But during those final months something else came to light: the monstrosity of the crimes perpetrated by the Nazi regime. As the concentration camps in Auschwitz, Bergen-Belsen, Buchenwald and Theresienstadt were liberated by the Allies, it dawned on the Germans that they had, wittingly or – mostly – unwittingly, been serving a wholly nefarious system. It brought rack and ruin to practically the whole continent, far beyond what might be considered the normal ravages of war. The most abhorrent deed, the killing of 6 million Jews in the death factories of the Holocaust, has brought shame on the German name which will remain with it until the end of history.

The Germans – with the remarkable exception of the former GDR – made an honest effort to come to terms fairly and squarely with this dark chapter of their past. They made amends as best they could by paying billions of Deutschmarks in terms of compensation, settling Jewish claims and individual demands. The former German territories east of the Oder-Neiße rivers, including East Prussia, were irrevocably ceded in the diplomatic run-up to reunification. German textbooks openly address the subject of Nazi crimes. And there have been recurrent waves of public debate: at the time of the Nuremberg war crimes trials; when Adenauer and Ben-Gurion agreed on restitution; during the Auschwitz trial in Germany and the Eichmann trial in Israel; in the wake of the student rebellion in 1968; when the American Holocaust series was shown on German television; most recently in 1994 when Steven Spielberg's *Schindler's List* was shown in cinemas.

Undeniably, there is a German consensus, rejected only by a minuscule group of extreme right-wingers, that remembrance is the secret of reconciliation – reconciliation with the victims of yesterday and their descendants as well as with our own history. The past will not go away, but it can be lived down by sincerity and good deeds.

The 8th of May 1945 remains an ambiguous and ambivalent historical date. It was the day of Germany's defeat and, at the same time, the day of Germany's liberation. The painful truth is that without this bitter defeat there would have been no liberation. The complete humiliation of the Nazi dictatorship was the prerequisite for the triumph of Germany's post-war democracy. Tyranny had to be vanquished for freedom to flourish. On this note, let me end with an observation made by Bertolt Brecht:

'Humankind has a remarkably short memory when it comes to suffering endured. Let us therefore keep on saying what has already been said so often. Let us keep on giving the same warnings – even if the words are like ashes in our mouths.'

PETER VON ZAHN

First Contacts with the British Army

My first encounter with British soldiers had a surrealistic quality. Hours before our capitulation in Kurland, Latvia, I decided that being a prisoner of the Red Army was not my cup of tea. Two days later, thanks to a minesweeper of the German Navy, I landed near Kiel. It was 11 May. The bay was filled with hundreds of German small craft. They had evacuated thousands, maybe hundreds of thousands, of German troops from all shores of the Baltic Sea between Finland and the Skagerak.

The soldiers went ashore in groups of fifty or so. They carried their knapsacks and rifles. From a small rowing boat I observed a rather unexpected scene. Before the Germans were marched off by British Royal Marines, they threw their rifles on the ground. The Marines picked them up with great effort and care, and, with bundles of German rifles under their arms, raced after their prisoners. They did not use their butt ends on them but tried to make the Germans carry their weapons themselves. This was vigorously refused. The struggle went on until I lost sight of the group.

In my radio days later on, I wrote many commentaries about the *Ohne mich* movement and the British and American attempts to recruit the Federal Republic into NATO. In retrospect, it seems that in the *Strander Bucht* near Kiel I had witnessed a preview of things to come. The next impression of the mood of the British soldier was given me during the following night by Sergeant-Major Brown of the Royal Marines. He was a stocky man with 17 years in the service; India, Dunkirk, El Alamein, fighting and marching from Normandy to the Baltic coast. He had liberated the Bergen-Belsen concentration camp and swore he would have shot every single SS man if it had been permitted by his superiors.

However, he bore no grudges against the German Army. He did not like his officers very much nor his government. He complained about sore feet and was looking forward to an early demobilization. It was a friendly talk we had that night. It ended with his good-natured wish, that 'they' would not send me to work in Russian camps. 'They' did not. By some quirk of luck, eight weeks later I was head of the Talks and Features department at Radio Hamburg, Military Government radio station.

Enemy Stereotypes and Perceptions

How did the victorious and the defeated soldiers assess each other? Under the circumstances, 'democracy versus fascism' was a mere catchphrase that did not help or explain much. The German soldiers were surprised to discover in the British Army visible traces of a traditional class society. In the defeated army, differences between officers and other ranks were less pronounced. As I mentioned, the English knew that the German Army and the SS had been following two different concepts of life and death. The Germans, by their efforts to surrender to British forces rather than to the Red Army, demonstrated how much they appreciated civilized standards of behaviour. Unlike today, relatively few Germans spoke English. Having fought for years in Russia, they were more familiar with Russian than with British attitudes. One should not forget the million or more men of the Vlassov army in German uniform.[2] Each German company had a few auxiliary orderlies – *Hiwis*, as they were known.

Because of this, or in spite of it, many German soldiers would have chosen to go on fighting the Red Army, had the Western Allies made the first move. In the prisoner-of-war camps in Holstein, which I knew well, this was the favourite subject of nightly discussions. It shows how naively they underestimated the emotional and practical ties which held the anti-Hitler coalition together.

Naturally, there was much bad feeling amongst the Germans because of the indiscriminate bombing of German cities and civilian targets by the Royal Air Force. But the British soldier was not held responsible for it. Perhaps Bomber Harris. Or Churchill. The German soldier blamed the Western governments, but even more his own government. He blamed the former because of their naivety in supporting the Russians while ruthlessly defeating Germany. In his eyes, however, Hitler had been guilty of sacrificing hundreds of thousands in a futile fight against the West instead of bolstering the front in the East.

There were some good reasons for Field Marshal Montgomery's edict against fraternization. But the ban on friendly contact with German girls and women was widely ridiculed by my British acquaintances. The control officers at Radio Hamburg disregarded it with gusto. Some Germans felt insulted. The younger women were disappointed. I could live with Montgomery's orders, being married to an English lady who openly fraternized with me. Long after the Field Marshal's proclamation was revoked, the problem appeared in North-West German Radio. Hugh Carleton Greene's secretary was a nice, good-looking British girl. She had an affair with one of our literary editors. This man had been a POW in England and was a communist. Some obscure British authorities sent him to Germany, together with three more communists, amongst them Karl-Eduard von Schnitzler. I am pretty sure that Hugh Greene knew something about his secretary's predilection and, like his brother, enjoyed the puzzle: who is spying on whom?

How did I judge the first actions of Military Government? The question should be answered on the basis of my experience as commentator, reporter and head of department at Radio Hamburg. The station was meant to be a conveyor belt for transmitting information from Military Government to the German population.

My task, as I understood it, was to explain British actions in a way that would build up trust amongst my German countrymen – trust in the validity of my interpretations and confidence in the intentions of the British administration. In the midst of destroyed cities, industries, communications and a hungry mass of people who had lost their homes and possessions, the task needed some optimism. The members of the British Control Group – a dozen officers with technical know-how and knowledge of Germany – were fully aware of the situation of the German staff. They saw that conditions in the occupied country were different from the assumptions with which they had been sent to Hamburg. Unnecessarily harsh measures were executed in a highly mechanical way, and in the case of the internment of the Ruhr industrialists, for example, had been provocatively justified by German war guilt, collective or otherwise. Our controllers feared that this line would be counterproductive and unhelpful in mobilizing the population for the really important things: repairing the damaged infrastructure, seeding and harvesting, digging coal for Europe, distributing food fairly.

The British staff agreed when we did not speak on the radio as if we were prosecutors, and avoided language that would have sounded outrageous to our countrymen. A certain degree of irreverence towards higher authority was tolerated and, after Hugh Carleton Greene arrived, even encouraged. By the autumn of 1945, we were criticizing certain actions of the occupying power. My colleague Axel Eggebrecht covered the Bergen-Belsen trial in all its gruesome detail every night after the news; on the evening the death sentences were pronounced he argued passionately against capital punishment.

During the first six months of occupation, I often found British Military Government very pragmatic in disregarding over-strict directives from above (if there were directives at all; for a time we had the feeling that North-West German Radio operated in a leaderless vacuum). In the end common sense prevailed.

When the radio stations in the three other zones were still under the strictest control, the German staff of North-West German Radio took on responsibilities that their colleagues in other zones could only dream of. The liberal regime of the Radio Control Unit attracted talent from every corner of Germany. The English staff, in competition with the German Service of the BBC, was proud of its success. Censorship was lenient and very soon reduced to a minimum. The manuscripts of ticklish commentaries, which should have gone through censorship before being broadcast, were never 'ready' until it was time for the officer in question to disappear into the officers' mess for dinner.

In respect of the screening of personnel, I shall describe my own case. I did not claim to be a resistance fighter. I was a run-of-the-mill war correspondent in the propaganda company of the 16th Army. I did not have a 'name', but I could write German talks with no traces of the Nazi idiom. I spoke fairly good English. All this was true, but did they check it? I believe not. Much later on I asked Captain Everitt, who hired me, whether he had any guidelines beside the fact that he was not to hire Nazis? Was there perhaps a recommendation by one of my English acquaintances from before the war, who happened to be a big shot in the Foreign Office? His answer was: 'Nothing of the sort. We simply liked your attitude. Besides, we could have thrown you out again at a moment's notice.'

In the three other zones similar action could not have been taken without lengthy, careful checks and screenings. The secret of North-West German Radio's success during the first years was the British administration's generous delegation of responsibility.

Cold War Background

In all my jobs during the war, I was able to keep myself fairly well informed about the international situation. After the entry of the United States into the war, I expected the defeat of the German armies. After Tehran, the partition of Germany seemed to me very likely. If I was surprised by developments, then it was by the suddenness with which the Allied war coalition broke in two. Tensions between the Soviets and the British were openly discussed by the officers of the British Radio Control Unit. They were quite outspoken in conversations with me. As they saw it the Potsdam Conference was a futile attempt to gloss over deep-seated and perhaps irreconcilable differences, particularly in Germany and about Poland.

On orders from higher up we were admonished not to dwell on quarrels between East and West. But when I was dispatched to Berlin in October 1945, I was encouraged to report the situation there factually and without distorting my opinions. Interviews with Pieck, Grotewohl and other influential Communist functionaries confirmed my impression of a planned Sovietization of the Russian Zone.

Leading functionaries of the German Communist Party (not yet the Socialist Unity Party) coolly discussed in my presence their intentions in respect to the Western zones of Germany. In an unrecorded interview, the chief-to-be of the Hamburg Communist Party, Mr Gundelach, said that control of the Ruhr was the ultimate aim of his and the Soviet side.

Six months after Germany's unconditional surrender, the Cold War on a global scale was undeniably on. Use of the atom bomb had not only ended the war in the Pacific but also set up signposts with 'No Trespassing', against further Soviet expansion. The Red Army was kept out of Japan. Quite a few people in Germany expected a violent East–West clash to break out when the Soviet Union refused to withdraw from Iran in early 1946. When they were forced to leave, this confirmed my conviction that from now on it would be American power that would have to be taken into account everywhere.

British information policy in Germany played this point down. In the press Montgomery ranged before Eisenhower, Bevin before Byrnes, Attlee before Truman. I saw this as one more reason for our commentaries to support the development of strong, if not yet clearly defined, ties between the new Germany and the West. It was the recipe for the future. And as such my outlook has not been changed by the events of the last 50 years. To strengthen Germany's ties with the West is just as valid a programme for political action now as it was in 1945. I will admit, however, that there were moments when I imagined the House of Windsor ruling over Hanover again. It was not quite high treason. Perhaps it was a mistake.

NOTES

1. This is an abridged version of a talk given at the Deutsch–Englische Gesellschaft Hamburg, published as 'From War to Democracy. British–German Relations in 1945 and 1995', in *3. Mai 1945. Erinnerung an das Kriegsende in Hamburg*, Hamburger Universitätsreden 56, Presse-Stelle der Universität Hamburg (Hamburg, 1996) pp 15–30. We are grateful to Lord Annan and the Deutsch–Englische Gesellschaft for kindly agreeing to its incorporation in this volume.

2. Commanded by Lieutenant-General Andrej Andrejewitsch Vlassov, the Vlassov army consisted of Soviet prisoners-of-war, and aimed to overthrow the communist regime in the Soviet Union (two divisions). In 1945 Vlassov was extradited by the Americans to the Soviet authorities.

1. B.U.5020 German woman giving coffee to two young British soldiers.

3. B.U.5190 British policeman, giving instructions to German policeman in Bremen. 2 May 1945.

2. OPPOSITE. B.U.5673 A British soldier keeps a watchful eye on the crowd in Lüneburg.

4. B.U.5376 Germans beside a 'Welcome' sign chalked on the bombed-out buildings. 4 May 1945.

5. B.U.7016 Citizens of Burgsteinfurt view film on concentration camps in Belsen and Buchenwald.

6. B.U.4636 Germans have to help bury the dead of an atrocity camp in Northern Germany.

7. B.U.5187 Germans reading news of Military Government on a board.

8. B.U.6200 British-German co-operation in delousing at Sandbostel concentration camp.

9. B.U.5668 Germans on market place of Lüneburg after hearing news of capitulation.

10. B.U.5137 Admiral v. Friedeburg in front of Field Marshal Montgomery's tent.

11. B.U.6711 The Dönitz Government is arrested. 23 May 1945.

12. B.U.6714 Speer, Dönitz and Stumpff after arrest, 23 May 1945.

13. B.U.5033 Germans flee behind the British lines.

14. B.U.4904 German prisoners-of-war being marched to the rear areas, 29 April 1945

15. B.U.4902 German prisoners-of-war being taken by the British.

16. E.A.65948 First newspaper (American) to print the news of capitulation.

6

Extracts from Contemporary Correspondence and Diaries

INTRODUCTION

These extracts from contemporary correspondence and diaries reflect both British and German views. The texts were written under the immediate impact of fighting and the first, often stark, encounters between victors and vanquished. They met as soldiers, as civilians, in their military capacity as well as that of observer. On the German side, the documents assembled mostly reflect the final phase of the war, although there are extracts from the post-surrender time as well. This circumstance is mainly due to the breakdown of postal services after defeat. In their combination of dogged persistence in the propaganda rhetoric of imminent achievable victory and traditional Christian beliefs, these letters document the process of psychological stress and dislocation experienced in the last weeks of the war.

The British letters and diaries concentrate to a larger degree on the perception of the enemy, drawing on preconceived notions of the Germans that were built up throughout the war. This perspective, however, is replaced by deep shock at the discovery of Bergen-Belsen, Buchenwald, Sandbostel and other concentration camps. Indeed, this is the point where the two sides lend themselves most readily to comparative analysis. Examples of this are the accounts by a British medical doctor and a German schoolgirl, both involved in medical work in Sandbostel concentration camp. On the whole, these extracts, written without any wider audience in mind, offer insights into the psychological impact of this time on contemporaries.

BRITISH CORRESPONDENCE AND DIARIES[1]

Captain Robert Barer MC: Letters to his wife

6 March 1945

It's been interesting to see the reactions of German civilians. Their plight is desperate and nearly every house has been damaged. I was asked by one woman to go and see a sick man. I descended into a dark cellar, wondering if I had walked into a trap, and found a damp and airless place on the floor of which slept 15 people – old men women and children in a space about the size of one of your rooms. There was an old man of 70 with lung trouble – probably hypostatic pneumonia. I did what I could for him – I managed to get him evacuated to hospital later – and as I went I heard a young girl say 'you see they are good people, they are not as we have been told'. I'm afraid I felt like crying – in fact I did afterwards. The trouble is that it's always the wrong people who suffer in war – not the really guilty ones. The children are beginning to overcome their fear and many of them play quite happily in the fields. One cannot help feeling that they have been 'liberated' from something worse than the people of occupied countries. The treatment of civilians has been quite fair and correct – probably far better than they expected. Nevertheless it's inevitable that there should be suffering and it's lucky that we're approaching summer, for if all German towns are to end up in the same state as those I've seen there'll be just nowhere to put people and we'll be getting epidemics...

Sandbostel, April 1945

...One morning the great news came. The Guards Armoured Division was going to liberate Sandbostel.... I have heard many apologists, both German and British, try to explain away conditions in concentration camps as being due to a breakdown of the supply system caused by bombing of transport and the approach of our troops. Sandbostel gives the lie to this excuse. There we had in one camp, on the one hand prisoners of war humanely treated, with no evidence of serious supply difficulties, and side by side with them political prisoners kept under conditions which beggar description. No words of mine can ever convey the full horror of what I saw there. A combination of Charles Dickens and Edgar Allan Poe might have done so, but I doubt it...

3 May 1945

...No words could possibly convey the horror of the place, yet some idiot has to tell a ridiculous lie about the Germans meaning to murder the 7,500 political prisoners. Actually the S.S. had left days ago & the shells were not aimed at the prisons anyhow.... I shall never forget Sandbostel. It was much smaller than Belsen but the individual suffering was the same.... now I would believe anything – absolutely anything. The S.S. are just not human – they must be exterminated. It would be far better to kill a few thousand innocent ones than allow a single one of them to escape.... a week ago I forced the German commandant of the ordinary POW camp to go round the political camp with me. At the end he said 'I must confess that at this moment I am ashamed to be a German'. I don't really think they knew about what went on in these places. However they are not the only ones to blame. I think one of the enclosed cuttings puts our share of the blame quite well. It makes me boil with rage to think that I should have been treated as a criminal for what I did in 1938-9. Even now I suppose people in England will not believe these things. They'll say the pictures are faked. No picture on earth could ever convey one millionth of the real horror. One felt no pity for these people – only loathing & disgust.

5 May 1945

Our guns fired the last salvo at 8 a.m. I suppose we shall have to fight another war on the political front. God knows how we are going to save any of Germany from the results of her criminal folly. In many ways they've got off very lightly despite the destruction of many of their towns and the huge loss of life. The people obviously have not the slightest idea of what the Nazis and S.S. have really done.... Every nation has the responsibility of knowing what is going on in its prisons and similar places and the Germans have shirked their responsibility.... We have seen the greatest degradation of the human race of all time and every one of us has become defiled ... the tragedy is that it should have happened in Germany – which has given so much to the world. Please forgive me for bothering you like this but I can think of nothing else at the moment...

8 May 1945

It would have been best if I'd poured petrol on the place and burned everything. I can still feel the stench in my nostrils. I'm quite sure that if every German were made to see these camps there would never be another war. You may be horrified at the pictures of German women being made to bury the dead but it's the best thing that could happen. They will never forget it. I am sure there has never been anything like it in the history of the world. The Middle Ages and Inquisition were probably humane by comparison. Well dear, I'm sorry this has been such a horrible letter but I had to get it off my chest and it's as well you should know...

Brigadier David Baines

4 May 1945

In action at Leer. The Germans surrender to Field Marshal Montgomery's 21st Army Group. Every anti-craft gun firing tracer in a tremendous feu-de-joie. The war was over.

6–18 May 1945

We relaxed first in a little German village called Klein Hesepe, north of Lingen, and then back in Holland, at Vorden near Nijmegen, where we had spent so many months of the war and had many friends.

18 May 1945

The battery moved to Weertzen, about 230 miles away, a little village near Zeven, north of the Hamburg–Bremen autobahn. Here we rejoined 30 Corps, listened to General Horrocks on the problems of sorting out Germany, and started armoured car and carrier patrols to try and control Russian labourers who were looting and murdering their former masters. We caught three setting fire to a farm one night, and I had to attend a British military government court at Bremervörde. A Russian officer came to defend them.

1 June 1945

The battery moved to Hamburg, and was in houses near the North Elbe bridge. The rule was very firmly 'no fraternization' and this was not easy to obey in that city, even though it was in ruins. The girls used to lie on the grass outside the men's cookhouse, and ask for food and cigarettes. Very tantalising. Clubs were started, and Harry Rolfe, who owned a dance band in civilian life, became secretary of the country club at Blankanese [sic], a fabulous place belonging to a German cigarette millionaire called Peters, with an indoor swimming pool and every possible luxury. At night we patrolled sectors of Hamburg, enforcing curfews and looking for Nazi party members. We were given a crafty little interpreter who pretended to know who was a Nazi but I think he was usually lying. If we found any books or papers or uniforms with swastikas on we took the head of the family off to prison. I was given an interesting job as a spare G SO 3 at the Hamburg headquarters, being able to speak a little German. I had to go and collect SS officers from the German divisions which were still in being up in Schleswig-Holstein and near Buxtehude, and take them to a British 'concentration camp' on the Elbe at Neuengamme. They thought they would be shot – perhaps they were.

The German headquarters still had their sentries in field boots and helmets, with rifles. Every single German staff officer seemed to own a female civilian secretary, which appeared very odd to me then, as all the English girls were in uniform as ATS or WRNS. The British intelligence staff were, if anything, even more of a shock to a naive young subaltern. Probably they were very good, but they obeyed no known rules, not that there were many, and 'non-fraternisation' certainly did not apply to their way of life. Our Mess was the 'Four Seasons' hotel on the Alster, quite undamaged, and even then a remarkable place. Apart from the area near the Alster the city was completely ruined, with tens of thousands buried under the rubble. Seeing the slow return to normal life in a city of that size was an unforgettable experience.

(Miss) M.E. Allan (War Correspondent)

Brussels, Thursday, no date: Letter to parents

...it has all been terribly interesting and I hope to do a bit of speaking when I get back to town. I shall tell everyone I meet about Belsen, for instance – people must know what the Germans have done and not flinch hearing. I went three times to Hamburg, each time surprised to find myself so much at the top of the map, so to speak. Our press camp was just like living in a Walt Disney film. It was a beergarten in the middle of a pine forest – but one couldn't explore the forest for fear of mines. Actually the mines were being collected and the forest rang periodically with loud explosions. I collected health – I feel fine with all the fresh air, for the windows were wide open at night and one couldn't but absorb it. It was in Belsen that I 'celebrated' the peace, a ghastly experience but one I am glad to have had, for the sake of knowing from firsthand experience just what criminals the Germans can be. The roads all over Germany are streaming with refugees of every nationality – including the ex Wehrmacht, the Luftwaffe and the Panzer boys on the way home after defeat – that was a grand sight. It was very queer I must say to be in Germany, in an enemy country. The Germans were vastly impressed with our armour – the thousands of vehicles of every kind, tanks, Bren gun carriers, jeeps trucks, etc. It is a very beautiful country, so beautiful that one all the more cannot forgive them for being the cruel people they are. If you can imagine a typical countryside, half English half Scottish, and multiplied ten times in size, that is something of the beauty of Northern Germany. Its size is impressive, and I was sceptical of all the lebensraum talk, since there was so much space. My conducting officer however pointed out how much of the country has poor soil. All the same it can grow magnificent forests – always useful for pitprops and paperpulp. Yes, I have no sympathy for the Germans.

6 May 1945: Letter to parents

...Whoever thought as we sat ... on a train to France & Belgium, that at that moment the germans were capitulating to the British ... It is very queer being in Germany & ... being able to smile at people ... the Belsen & Buchenwald revelations have shaken us all. I saw the 3 Newsreel films ... I do beg you to go and see them, for the sake of seeing what the Germans are capable of and for telling other people....

Notebook: Background on Germany

...Dogged persistence, endurance & stamina of the German people.... The 1939–4? war is a deadly game in which the employment of economic resources, wealth & armaments, with a maximum of energy, determination, courage, heartless efficiency & soulless cunning, will decide the ultimate verdict.... Nazi Germany – a crazy structure built upon fear and force.... War is madness, without objective, without good result, without sense, without morality, without justice, and without mercy.... Nazis, young & old of both sexes, ardently & genuinely believe that war is glorious & desirable; that peace is demoralising; that racially superior Germans must drive out the Jews from Germany; that the Nazi Reich is an ideal state for which the good German should be happy to die or kill ruthlessly; that extreme Nationalism is the guiding force of a new era ... Nevertheless there are thousands of German hearts whose glow has diminished perceptibly since the outbreak of war in 1939 ... men & boys of military age to whom war now appears less glamorous than it had been portrayed to their primitive & unspoiled minds. In many German hearts the flame of faith is flickering. Parents find their children taught not only to hate the Jews, but to rebel against Church & home.

The winning of the peace: background on Germany

...Must heal from insides rid of the Germ [*sic*] – not 'Hitlerism'; it is someth [*sic*] even worse than that – I am alluding to the pernicious Combine of Reichswehr & Big Business. – must smash the economic power of the industrial magnates and armament kings on the Rhine & Ruhr...

Lieutenant-Colonel Henry Crozier: Diary

2 May 1945

Eventually crossed the Elbe at 1400 hs and moved to a large Explosives factory at Grunhof.... 11 Arm'd Div have captured Lübeck and 6 Airborne have reached the Baltic. Berlin has fallen to the Russians. Von Busche [*sic*] is coming through our lines tomorrow morning to discuss surrender with the Army Commander...

3 May 1945

After a fantastic day of negotiations with high ranking German officers, Hamburg formally surrendered at 1800 hs. We are not marching in tonight but going in at first light tomorrow...

4 May 1945

Today we entered Hamburg and occupied the town. All resistance has ceased and the whole Northern German Army Group including Denmark has surrendered. The Bn has the fantastic job of putting picquets all round the city, about 1½ times the size of Glasgow! We have to disarm the German Army, enforce the curfew, house & sort out thousands of released allied Pw of all nationalities & displaced persons without houses. Quite the worst job I've ever had & far worse than any battle!...

5 May 1945

The Bn gathered in arox. [*sic*] 3,000 Pw alone today! In addition we had over 2,500 Russians, Poles, French etc. and large numbers of slave workers to sort out. The Germans are proving very amenable to discipline and there have been no incidents...

9 May 1945 Wednesday

VE day and the war in Europe is finished! Just 11 months since the start of the 'Normandy' Campaign – It will go down in history as one of the model campaigns of all time. I don't feel like celebrating – I can't help thinking of the colossal task in front of us and of the awful sights I've seen in Germany & all over Europe. It will take a life time to get back to normal...

10 May 1945

We continue to pick up Every type of person in Europe, German PW, allied PW ... and thousands of homeless wanderers – we got a good haul today by catching Seyss Inquhart [sic]! A foul specimen – wonder what will happen to him...

Sergeant W.J. Barclay

Report written in Belsen concentration camp (liberated 13 April 1945)

Belsen. It is the 21st April in the year of civilization 1945. The light is fading at the close of a day of rain & sun intermingled.... I am sitting in the concentration camp at Belsen, Germany. Three days since the name Belsen meant nothing to me but after today it will be indelibly printed on my mind. The platoon has brought supplies three hundred & fifty miles to this camp and if this was the only work they had done, they have justified their existence. Picture a wild stretch of country comprising sand dunes covered with coarse grass & stunted bushes, here and there lumps of pine trees with an occasional stretch of grassland. The whole area surrounded by a barbed wire fence divided in three enclosures known as camps I, II & III.... Within these areas are confined 60,000 prisoners, men, women and children. Many are without shelter and live in holes in the ground. Sanitation is almost non-existent, there is no running water & no lighting. Clothing is of the scantiest and no bedclothes are allowed. The inmates are political prisoners and hostages, and comprise Germans, Russians, Belgians, French, Dutch, Czechs and every other nationality in Europe, including four Englishmen.... Most of the prisoners were ordinary, decent people, just like ourselves, who have become enmeshed in this most horrible of systems.

They are now little more than animals. It was decided a time ago to eliminate the prisoners by starvation and disease. Typhus rages through the camp and the inmates have not the strength or in many cases the will or wish to combat it. As with most evils, the results were beyond imagination and the thing got completely out of hand. Between 400 and 600 people died daily and despite burial squads & a crematorium they died faster than the bodies could be disposed of. The camp was guarded by Hungarian soldiers ... while the actual keepers were stormtroopers both men & women. The brutalities were almost beyond comprehension. Children had the fingers of their hands broken, men & women were beaten & worked until they dropped dead ... hangings & executions were every day occurrences. The prisoners had to carry the dead to the burial pits and were often too weak to move away in which case they were pushed in with the dead. Over all hung the plague of typhus. When our troops were within striking distance the Governor of the camp asked for a truce that we might take it over intact. We agreed, providing the guards were left intact. After quibbling this was agreed to and we took the whole lot over, prisoners, guards & SS.

When we took over, most of the prisoners had had neither food nor water for five days. There were 5,000 unburied dead. The living were stripping the dead of their clothes to obtain more warmth for themselves, using the bodies for pillows, and were eating the flesh from the dead. All the records of the inmates had been destroyed and the task confronting us was superhuman.... The S.S. have to do the dirty work each under armed guard who make sure that the job is done at the double & done properly. Women S.S. have the same treatment as the men. A bayonet jab is a useful spur to energy.... You will probably be pleased to hear that the S.S. are now in the same boat as the prisoners. Typhus has started on them & that combined with overwork has started to reduce their numbers...

The Reverend Cecil Cullingford

900 miles through Germany, no date

...I have returned from a tour of the fronts in Germany.... What has struck one most has been the general air of prosperity and well-being.... The other thing most noticeable is the complete lack of men, except for the very old or a few cripples. There seems to be a much larger population of slave workers, Russians, Poles, Belgians, Lithuanians, Dutch, women as well as men. The people of Germany have not needed to work hard, with so much slave labour to use for all purposes.... Fortunately at last they are getting their deserts.... In most cases they [the slave labourers] are taking their revenge. Some are going about in organised bands.... Our security section had to intervene to prevent them from lynching a farmer who, after declaring that he had no firearms, was taking five ... pistols to the woods where 5 SS men were known to be hiding. There is a good deal of rape going on, and those who suffer have probably well deserved it. Bremen was empty of German civilians – the bombing was too dangerous for them – but full of Russian slaves whose lives did not matter. These were either pushing barrows with barrels of beer or rolling through the streets with bottles in their hands. Our men, who now have seen, or know all about, the unspeakable horrors of Belsen and numbers of similar camps: who have found the hospitals in POW camps full of our own men – the survivors of those who were marched from Poland to the North Sea in the depth of winter without food, all who fell out for any reason being shot where they lay – without hands or feet as the result of frostbite from the march: they were not inclined to feel sentimental about the Germans, and are not particularly impressed when Germans come to them as if they were responsible for the Russians being there.... The last good hunting-ground was at Lüneburg! In barracks, full of white dress shirts and fur coats for the Russian campaign, were the shoulder badges I sent you. I also got a Primus stove which is proving useful.... The German Army in defeat is a disgusting sight – broken looking men who stink! It is unpleasant to pass a column; and we provide them with baths. Now there is the difficult job of governing Germany, and trying to make her a civilised nation again. There are no men left in the country, for they were all in the Army, and their places taken by the foreign slave workers. They all look fat, well fed and well clothed, far better than you do at home. Obviously all these years they have gone short of nothing: all the interesting things that we have had to do without they have had in plenty. But it is changed now. In all the towns there are enormous queues outside the food shops. There are practically no signs as yet of sabotage or 'Werwolf' activity, as we feared, and as the Germans had planned. The defeat of the Huns was so complete and so swift that they did not have time to organise the resistance they had planned: and even the Nazis probably saw that it would have been no use...

Lieutenant-Colonel William Brownlie

16 April 1945, Soltau-Celle region

...Near the farm where I was sitting was a sort of barbed wire cage, surrounding a hut. I broke down part of the fence, and was amazed to find over a dozen men and women of various nationalities, some French, ragged and in squalid conditions. They were slave workers who had been there for two or three years, and they 'belonged' to the farmer, who locked them in at the end of each day's work. They then ate what was passed through the wire. I got all this out of them, astonished at their casual and matter-of-fact description of their lot: they were totally dispirited and submissive, but I felt quite otherwise. I hauled out the farmer and his family, and made them tear all the wire down, no tools allowed. The ex-slaves sat and watched, smoking our cigarettes after eating a hot meal from our rations, and visibly came alive again. We had passed within two or three miles of Belsen, not seen it but heard about it, and the liberation of this miniature concentration camp gave me great satisfaction...

[Proceeding to a village called Poitzen] The wood was half a mile away, astride the road. A German half track had just emerged from it, and been destroyed. We had no infantry, so the best tactic was to go flat out, and circle the wood just out of Panzerfaust range: all quiet. I got permission to go further, and had a good view of a smaller wood to the right. There were movements, and two tiny white dots appearing at ground level: evidently men in split trenches. I put in four or five HE [high explosives], then a stream of MG [machine-gun fire].

The place took fire. Figures emerged waving white cloths, and I motored nearer. To my horror, they were civilians, followed by a horse and cart on which were piled all kinds of household goods. I halted a hundred yards from them, not knowing what else to do. Two figures came towards me. They were children, a boy and a girl, holding hands and running as hard as they could over the rough ploughed earth. They came right up to the tank, looked up at me, and the small boy said in English: 'You have killed my father.' There was nothing I could say. The only thing to do was to get on with the job.

Lieutenant W.A. Greene

Continental Journey: Being one man's account of a memorable journey made by thousands in 1944–45 through Normandy, France, Belgium, Holland and Germany [based on daily letters, typed in 1958] ... *Chapter Twenty-Five: The Victory Celebrations.*

Tuesday 8 May

An historic day. The first newspaper I picked up, the *News Chronicle*, called itself a Victory Issue and carried banner headlines: TODAY IS V DAY. CHURCHILL SPEAKS AT 3 P.M.; THE KING AT 9: TODAY AND TOMORROW ARE NATIONAL HOLIDAYS. How we had longed to see such news in the papers. Now we were satisfied. We had not had time to analyse our feelings. Somehow we took it all very calmly.... At 3 p.m. we listened to the Prime Minister's statement. So that was that. History had repeated itself. Germany, that fertile, progressive country, with so much in her favour, who had allowed herself once again to be dominated by powerminded leaders, had bitten the dust. In the soldier's phrase, she had 'had it'. Still nobody thought of work... Life was good; life was full: life was sweet...

GERMAN CORRESPONDENCE AND DIARIES[2]

Bruno S.

1 April 1945, Easter Sunday, Salesel üb. Aussig

If only this mess were all over, my darling. There is not really much left to say about it. But I refuse to believe that we did it all for nothing, that simply cannot be true. We will go on praying to God that fate might grant us victory after all.

If only I could be with you all...

Anon.

4 April 1945, Hamburg

Since this morning the *Volkssturm* [People's Army] has been mobilized here. If the situation doesn't change soon, you won't be getting much more post from me.... In case we don't see each other again ... after all, it's always possible that we will be cut off ... look after yourselves. Stay healthy, and don't come under the Bolsheviks.... Our local branch leader no longer needs to write to his wife. She is already with the Tommies.... In my view, regardless of the situation in the west, the counter offensive will come in the east. They don't constantly fly to the Mark Brandenburg for nothing...

I never thought that it would come to this. We had to accept that our borders would be endangered; the fact that the Rhine was not a barrier was bitter; and that the Siegfried Line did not live up to expectations was bitter too. Much has changed in four years. But don't give up hope. The picture can always change again...

Leutnant [Sub-lieutenant] Heinz L.

4 April 1945, Stab/SS – Prop. Unternehmen Skorpion

So I wanted to write to you again, perhaps the bitterest letter of my life ... The radio is dreadful! ... It can broadcast the worst news, and then play light dance music as if nothing had happened, not this fate which, I believe, is treating us so unjustifiably harshly. In some moments of doubt I want to ask God what we, who only wanted to serve the good and the beautiful, did to deserve this.

Hptm. [Captain] Paul D.

28 April 1945, 'Immelmann' Strack b. Milowitz

Time is passing unbelievably quickly, and not in our favour. A yawning abyss is opening under the German people. After they looked over the peak, they slowly descended into the depths, as if they were abseiling. So long as the Wehrmacht stays in step with the *Führer* in the lead, the Germans can keep the rope under control. But the moment that the battle for Berlin is over, in which, as things are, the *Führer* will find his nemesis, there will be no more question of a slow descent.

Dr Elfriede Leseberg

13 June 1945, Göttingen

Dear Mother,
 I hope that you will receive this letter very soon and find out that my return journey worked out well.... In Langelsheim I got on my heavily loaded bicycle and cycled along the Harz to Seesen, or rather, I had to push a lot because of the hills. From S. I got a lift for 10 kilometres in a trailer. Parts of that leg of the journey were a descent into Hell ... sometimes I didn't know where to hang on.... Exactly 12 hours after I had left Bassum we dawdled into Gö, sunburned and tired, but jolly glad that everything had gone so well.... All my things are here, even the case I left in the Institute of Ethnology, which, like many other Institutes, is protected by a sign saying 'Off limits to all troops'. So far only houses in the eastern quarter have been requisitioned. For example, a large picture of Stalin, framed with red flags, hangs resplendent in front of Ruprecht's house in the Herzberger Landstraße. So far Americans have been here, more recently the English. The Russian

border is not very far away, as Stalin has claimed Thuringia and Saxony as well. V[andenhoeck] & R[uprecht], an enterprising publisher, is already preparing an English dictionary and has all sorts of plans.

Gefr. [Lance-corporal] S.-F.: Diary

2 May 1945

It has been announced that Hitler is dead and that Grand Admiral Dönitz has taken over the Supreme Command. It is most unpleasant to be dependent on inadequate news just at this time.

Uffz. [NCO] Dr Heinrich V.: Diary

2 May 1945, Rewentiz near Prague

Morning news: the *Führer* has died in Berlin. Deep impression. Long silence. Clear shock. Helplessness. Dönitz successor. Appeal: the resistance goes on ... thereafter escape plans are discussed in detail. Afternoon: Ribbentrop has resigned, Count Schwerin-Krosigk successor. The President of the International Red Cross is said to have gone to Sweden to conduct negotiations.... The troops see the death of the *Führer* ... in a positive light as a heroic gesture. At least the majority do. The press and the radio ... set the tone.

3 May 1945, Rewentiz

The wife of our *Fähnrich* [cadet sergeant] ... works for the security services in the Protectorate, department of compulsory resettlement. She was involved in working on the expulsion of thousands of Jews from Prague. She speaks of the huge Jewish camp in Prague that still houses 30,000 Jews. Well, I hope they blow it up – Germany! German women! Nothing distances people so far from their human nature as being involved in committing crimes.... Comments made among friends show repeatedly that recent events have not produced the necessary political understanding. Few have gone through a Copernican change of heart. It is the thoughtful ones who now say openly what they have long been starting to think. The 'believers' will not change their views from one day to the next, although they naturally behave opportunistically and want to escape the consequences of the situation in any way possible. To drive out the views that have taken hold of them will be a long job. Politically this generation will be dead for ever, and must be so.

Eveline B.: Diary

6 May 1945, Celle

...we are so happy that we still have a German broadcasting station and can hear Germans and German news. Enemy broadcasting stations are so dreadful, starting from the way the announcers speak. Today the children and I thought about what greeting they should use now. As they didn't know, they have not been using any greeting at all. I told them that they could go on saying 'Heil Hitler' because Hitler had been the *Führer* to the end. But if they felt uncomfortable about it, they could say 'good day' or 'good morning'...

Käthe T. to Werner K.

1 April 1945

I wanted to write to you a couple of days ago, but we have had two more serious air raids, which lasted a long time. As a result, we are especially busy at work. Also we have no water again, and as you can imagine, that also creates more work for us.... In the evenings we can't do much either because then we have air raid warnings that last for a few hours. I have to help Mother with the work much more now, otherwise the housework simply isn't done. Mother always has to queue for a long time for the little food that we can buy. Yes, my dear Werner, much has changed over the last few months.... Believe me, I should like to marry, and your dreams and plans match mine. Only it can't happen so quickly because

Mother and Father must first be persuaded that one is entitled to make the occasional mistake in life.... Today at lunch everyone was so sad again. Who knows, in three weeks' time they might already be fighting for Hamburg. Where should we go? The food is getting worse all the time, and there is hardly enough...

Anon.[3]

Görlitz, 2 February 1945

I am terribly worried about what will become of you in Berlin.... If only I had sent you the things that I intended to take to you. But straight after that no more packets were accepted. I couldn't have sent potatoes – they would have arrived frozen. Do you have enough? ... We have been under great pressure for a few days, and hope that the greatest danger for Görlitz is over for the moment. Everyone here is very nervous and excited. We had already discussed everything in case we have to flee. Louise's message that we could go to Bremen came just at the right time. We can take only what we can carry. It would be dreadful if we had to leave everything behind.... We now have nine strangers in our rooms. Eight of them are refugees, all adults. I had to rearrange the whole flat and empty the wardrobes within 24 hours.... Görlitz is said to have 100,000 refugees. Yesterday the figure was as high as 110,000...

Your Mother

Anon.

3 April 1945, Unterlüss

My beloved Kuniang!

Your phone call yesterday afternoon helped me more than you know ... seeing Mother and Father again in the most primitive surroundings without the simplest things necessary for life, finding Mother thinking of leaving this earthly vale of tears ... all this naturally also affected me deeply.... In the end we all agreed that our relatives should stay where they are, and I also think it was right for Helga to stay in Kronberg.

Elfie Walther: Diary

28 April 1945, evening

I have just received my conscription papers. An English officer and a German came and brought me the letter. I am to be in front of the Town Hall tomorrow morning at seven, with things for several days. They want to send us away. Mother thinks that we might be deployed as foreign workers. I don't believe it. We are much too young.

1 May

We have been told that we are to clear up a camp near Hamburg. I got a dreadful shock and had to think of the pictures at home. A concentration camp! I had heard enough about them over the last few days. I hope we don't have to go into the camp with all the dead people, I thought...

In Wildeshausen we saw traces of the battle. Houses burnt down everywhere, burned-out cars and tanks. Between Bassum and Harpstedt we went past a huge camp of tents. There seem to be Russians and Poles there. They were setting about burning all sorts of things. Some of them stood by the side of the road and shook their fists at us. They called abuse after us. We were afraid, and hoped that the car would drive past quickly. But to our horror, it stopped, and we had to get out amidst the taunts and shouts of the foreigners. It was driven home to me how it is to be afraid of violence. My heart was in my mouth.

Suddenly we saw a large POW camp. Once again Russian soldiers were standing behind the fences and staring at us. That was Sandbostel, south of Bremervörde. We turned off and drove to another corner of the camp. There were huge barracks there. We were told to clean out these barracks and prepare them for political prisoners from a concentration camp who were camping nearby. First we had to clean out a barrack for ourselves...

After we had made the barracks reasonably clean, we moved in. There are two sacks of straw between three of us. Now we are sitting here and waiting for further instructions. And for something hot to eat! For days we have not had a square meal. All we have had is the bread that we brought with us, and chocolate which the English gave us.

1 May 1945, late in the evening

I have just heard the most terrible news. I must write it down today. We have one candle, so it's possible...

In the hospital barrack there were three old medical orderlies from the time when the camp had housed POWs. We stayed there for a while and asked them questions. Then they started to tell us things that gave us shivers down the spine. I can hardly repeat them, it is so incredible! But I will try in a few words. When the guards from the POW camp had disappeared SS soldiers brought prisoners from a concentration camp. Where it was, the orderlies didn't know. The prisoners were in incredibly bad condition, half dead, half starved.

They were driven out of the railway wagons or tipper trucks – I didn't quite understand this – with bayonets. They were beaten and stabbed with the bayonets. According to the orderlies, the SS treated them dreadfully. Most of the prisoners remained lying where they were unloaded. They could hardly walk, staggered, fell. Then suddenly the SS disappeared because the British were advancing. They just left the poor people lying there in the rain and dirt.

And that is how the British found them. They had to have help and people to look after them as quickly as possible. That is why they had the idea of getting schoolgirls in – and that is why we are here. Tomorrow we will have to wash and clean up the prisoners! Then they are to move into the barracks that we have cleaned. The orderlies didn't know any more that this...

I am dreadfully mixed up. Can this be true? If it is as the orderlies have told us, then the pictures of Bergen-Belsen are certainly true too. And what else might there be that we have no idea of? Is this what our soldiers were fighting for? Is this what the German people have been suffering for? Those pigs were lying to us, and now we have to bear the consequences! I am terrified of tomorrow. What will happen tomorrow? No one will be able to sleep here tonight. Everyone is speechless and listens to our report with unbelief.

2 May 1945

...Nobody at home would believe us if we told them about it. I couldn't stop thinking about how we had loved and honoured the

Führer. Everything that he told us was a lie! What is this thing that was called National Socialism? We always thought that it was something beautiful and noble.

Why is everything so cruel? Why do they kill innocent, helpless people? One can't treat one's enemies like that! It is incomprehensible. Last night I finished with everything that I used to believe was good. People are vile pigs – all of them, all of them, including me. And there is meant to be a God? And he allows all this to happen? ... I haven't seen a prisoner yet, and I notice that I am glad. I am frightened of seeing them. How can we apologize?...

4 May

Today we cleaned out another two barracks. So much dirt! We can't wash at all, and look like pigs. When we asked an English officer if we could wash somewhere he snapped at us not to put on such airs and graces. The prisoners had not been able to wash for years. I believe we already have lice...

4 May, evening

I was happy too soon. It is cruel in the typhus barracks. I lack the right words to describe all the misery. They are hardly people. Skeletons lie there in their filthy beds, smeared with excrement from head to foot, and stare at us with huge eyes.... How ashamed I am in these minutes to be German! We caused this! And my mother does not believe that Germans could do something like this!

5 May 1945

When can we go home? There are so many rumours. We have heard that Hitler is dead. And all the others. Himmler is said to have been captured. I wonder if the war is over everywhere.... Today two men died. We had to carry them out. Some never open their eyes. They just lie there and moan. Sometimes there is no sound any more. Then the others say he is dead. When we dragged the dead men out, the others immediately pounced on their few personal belongings. Their feelings have been dulled...

I had never seen a dead person before. Today I had to carry two. When the first one died I could not control myself and broke down in tears. He was a Greek. At the end his breath rattled and he kept beating the wall with his fists. When the other patients who could stand saw me crying, they smirked. They have seen so much, death does not mean much to them anymore. And the British had their satisfaction when they saw that we didn't know what to do. One has the feeling that they want to punish us because we are Germans. Understandable...

6 May 1945

More and more sick people are being brought in. There are 6 barracks in our complex, and all are overcrowded. Another 600 new patients are to be brought today. But yesterday and today more than 100 people died.

In total, an English soldier told me, there are more than 3,000 people in the camp...

Our mental state is much worse than our physical condition. We will never lose these impressions. What we experience here cannot be described in words...

Evening

This afternoon I was close to despair. Inge has dropped out too, and I have to do all the work in our barracks alone. As everything takes longer, some of the patients become quite aggressive, and I was really scared. Thank goodness there is also a room with nice, educated people in it. They come from Holland and Belgium. Some of them are doctors, and then there is a lawyer, he always consoles and encourages us.

Just imagine: someone who has suffered so much at the hands of our people encourages us! He says that what we are doing here is wonderful. But, he says, it is shameful that people who are still half children have to put in order the mess that adults have created. All this man did was to make a comment against the German occupation in Holland. For this, he was taken to a concentration camp...

7 May 1945

...The suffering here is so dreadful. Sometimes I think I can no longer bear it. So many die. Wrapped in blankets, these skeletons walk – or rather, stagger – between the barracks. There really are children – gypsy children – among them. I can't understand it! They even put children in concentration camps!

Many of us are seriously sick. The British seem to be worried. Up to now they have taken little notice of how the German schoolgirls are. We have lice and are dirty. Many of us have no changes of clothes. Our coats and jackets are wet through because it is always raining, and our shoes are soaked and completely filthy...

8 May 1945

...Some women from the village helped peel the potatoes. They could give us some news from outside. The war is said to be over. Foreigners – I mean foreign workers – are living under dreadful conditions in the villages. I wonder if my parents are still alive? I am terribly worried. Men and women from the village have to bury the dead. We just put them outside the door. They are buried in a mass grave. An old woman who was crying all the time sat next to me.

When another woman cursed the SS and said that they would all be shot now, the woman next to me started to scream dreadfully and suddenly cut her artery with her potato knife. We were all frozen with terror. Someone called for help. The Frenchmen came from the kitchen, bandaged her arms, and took her away.

Later we were told that this woman had a son who had been in the SS. And when she heard that all SS people were to be shot, she did not want to live any longer. Her husband had died in the war. What fates people have!...

10 May 1945

We are leaving tomorrow! Quite suddenly! I can hardly believe it. After lunch our replacements arrived, 100 girls from Bremen. They didn't even have any luggage with them – they thought they were just going to look at a camp. Well, they'll have a good look round!

11 May 1945

I am home again, after a two-hour journey. In spite of the curfew in Delmenhorst, we ran home from the market place. My parents could not speak for joy. While we were away, nobody knew where we were.

...It is nice to be at home, but it is different from how it was before. I have experienced too many dreadful things. One needs time to cope with it.

I haven't told anybody anything, although everybody asks all the time. I simply can't yet. Perhaps I am afraid that they won't believe me?

Postscript

Soon after, at least twenty-five of my school friends went down with typhus, including my friend Rosi. We were injected afterwards. But for many it was too late. Three days after my return, everyone in my house had lice.

My parents were speechless when, one evening, I told them about the horrors. A world collapsed for them too, and at that time we didn't even know that everything I had seen was nothing compared with what had happened in other camps, and especially the extermination camps.

Max B.: Diary

Saturday 21 April 1945, Berlin

I reached the Charlottenburger Chaussee again in safety. In the meantime it has started to rain fairly heavily, and I cross the square of the Platz der Siegessäule. Soldiers are driving cattle out of the zoo across the square to safety – an unusual sight, a response to the worsening military situation. Soon I reach the two large bunkers. In the last few days propaganda slogans have been painted on their fronts in large white letters. 'Better dead than a slave!' I read on one, and 'Our honour is loyalty!' on the other. This is obviously intended to demonstrate the occupants' courage and determination to fight on. I can see a lively military group around the bunker. Obviously they are expecting to be besieged, and are getting in supplies of everything necessary, mainly ammunition and food. Soon I reach my flat. I go out on the balcony, and establish that the growling thunder of cannon fire is already audible in the south of the city as well. Presumably the Russians will surround the city, or attack from several directions, as they have done with all large towns so far.

Wednesday, 2 May 1945

And indeed, when I look down at the street and all around – a wonderful peace over everything! ... But yet ... 2 cannon shots from the Zoo bunker ... and another 2 straight away ... so, they are still shooting! ... But apart from that, peace far and wide! ... a ceasefire? ... Can it be possible? ... Inconceivable!! ... Just the occasional single shot – and no planes to be seen far and wide, whereas usually at this time, and especially when the weather is as clear as it is today, whole swarms of them cross the skies. Peace on the street, too, just the odd Soviet soldiers, in twos or threes ... and then ... I hear a public announcement made over loud-speakers from the direction of the Kurfürstendamm, first in Russian and then in German. It is generally unclear because it is so far away, and I can't understand anything except the words 'der Führer', repeated several times!... Something decisive must have happened! ... Something fundamental must have changed in the conduct of the war. Has just Berlin surrendered, or the whole Reich?... Down in the court, various bits of the announcement have been heard, and the wildest rumours are going around. They are saying that the Führer has shot himself, with his wife ... Goebbels and Ribbentrop, it is said, have been captured by the Russians, and the last stand, led by Hans Fritzsche – the Nazi radio commentator – has collapsed in Berlin, where he is said to have taken over the Supreme Command at the end. But there is still shooting from the Zoo bunker at lunchtime. Yes, Colonel Renner, that sad hero of 20 July 1944, is said to have entrenched himself there, wanting to fight on. In the afternoon, however, we heard that the Russians had penetrated the bunker ... and the cannon fire from the bunker did, in fact, stop at that time.

...They are accompanied by a young Red Army soldier who, they say, had helped them very politely, especially to cross the street, which wasn't so easy, and also to carry water. He joins us in the entrance hall, salutes, and shakes everybody's hand, crying 'Voina kaput! Voina kaput!' ... The war is over! ... I can hardly believe my ears at this almost unbelivable, <u>marvellous</u> news, and ask him, almost overcome by the greatness of the moment, whether it can be true? He confirms it again, and a broad grin of joy lights up his whole face. He must be a true friend of peace, for only such a one could thus express his joy that this greatest horror of our times is over.

All day long the people who live in this building are in a state of excitement about what is going to happen, coming to terms with the situation, about the <u>joy</u> of at last getting rid of the Nazis, who had more or less cast their accursed spell over everyone. Yes, the spell seemed to have been broken, and confessions could be freely heard from all sides ... suppressed for years and held back out of advisable caution ... about what people had thought about that violent lot who constantly threatened to annihilate anyone who did not agree with them. Here in this building ... I honestly believe this ... there was <u>nobody</u> who ever belonged to them, or who felt themselves to be one of them.

Clerks, workers, businessmen, who perhaps, at the start, might have gone along with them, but who soon saw that the wool was gradually being pulled over their eyes, that their complaisance was being exploited, so that they were soon embittered and just went along, or were forced to join in. While they cannot all be completely absolved from all complicity, in by far the majority of cases they were the victims purely of their political inexperience, their bourgeois complacency, and their trust in lying, exaggerated propaganda, so that they were soon incapable of seeing or distinguishing the true connections between world events...

The war – at least for us here in Berlin – was <u>over</u>! We had peace and quiet, whatever might happen in the future – the worst was over. It could hardly get worse than it had been, and in this spirit, more or less apathetically, we awaited what lay in store for us, developments which were just beginning. Only peace and quiet, no more grenades, and no bombs ... that alone was like a true liberation from all the previous evil, however much one might still have been affected by the past. This outweighed all other feelings.

Stabsarzt [Captain, Medical Corps] Dr M.: Diary

April 1946, Camp Neumünster

The fact that I, of all people, am counted among the 50,000 most prominent Nazis that they feel obliged to identify in the British Zone amuses me.... My last commandant, after all, warned his officers about my critical – to put it mildy – attitude to National Socialism. How can one believe in any justice and in the wish of people to create a better world. The Nazis did not want to, and neither do the Allies. Otherwise it would be simply unthinkable to treat a conquered people in this way. With the exception of the alleged mass murders, all the large and small abuses that are leading to convictions in the present concentration camp trials are being repeated now in the English concentration camps. All those who knew the German concentration camps in normal times repeatedly point out that the conditions under which we live here are much worse than they were then. I cannot judge that, but I know that the conditions here are unbelievable.

NOTES

1. All extracts are from individual manuscript collections held at the Department of Documents, Imperial War Museum, London.
2. Extracts are from manuscripts held at the Library of Contemporary History, Stuttgart, Lebensdokumentensammlung, Sammlung Feldpost 1945 (Letters from the Front Collection). All translations by Dr Angela Davies.
3. Ibid, vol 196.

7

Contemporary Documents and Broadcasts

INTRODUCTION

The documents included in this chapter draw attention to ideas that were discussed internally in the Foreign Office. By no means undisputed within these circles, they nevertheless reflect one, very expressive, strand of opinion. Often these texts show strong signs of 'Vansittartism', and they can be placed within the context of the transition stage at the end of the war, which was in many respects still anchored in the planning phase for occupation.

The documents should be read in conjunction with the essays on post-war planning (Kettenacker) and national stereotypes (Nicholls) in order to provide a more detailed background and evaluation in contemporary thought and public opinion. Especially the document entitled 'German Reactions to Defeat', first made available to scholarship and analysed by Lothar Kettenacker, should be seen as an example of pronounced statements regarding Germany, sparking off discussion and disagreement by Foreign Secretary Anthony Eden regarding Germany's predilection towards the East. Other texts found their way indirectly into the forming of attitudes in the occupation years, as in the case of the memorandum entitled 'The German Character', which was circulated amongst future occupation officers. Like the newspaper reportage on long-term developments, these documents link the evaluation of Nazi mentalities with earlier attitudes. In this they point back at least to the trauma of the First World War and the Versailles Treaty. All in all, these documents reflect to some extent the 'official mind'.

GERMAN REACTIONS TO DEFEAT[1]

Memorandum by the Secretary of State for Foreign Affairs

Top Secret
War Cabinet, 10 January 1945

I circulate to my colleagues a paper on 'German Reactions to Defeat'...

2. This study of the German mentality and its possible development in the future has been prepared by a member of the Foreign Office who knows Germany well. Any paper on so speculative a subject must be controversial, and I am not myself in agreement with all its conclusions; in particular I am not convinced that Germany will necessarily turn East rather than West, though the danger of this admittedly exists.

3. Clarity of mind and strength of will in this country will be of more importance in maintaining our security against Germany than any development in that country's own mind or will. For some time after her defeat we may, if we wish, be able largely to ignore what Germany thinks and feels. But we shall be able to do so less and less as time passes; and I hope therefore that this paper may serve as a useful estimate of one factor in the most crucial of our long-term problems.

Foreign Office, 10 January, 1945. AE.

Annex

When Germany has been beaten we shall find there a surprising chaos of ideas and beliefs, of political and personal aims. National faith will be dormant; the idea of the Reich will seem dead. Germans will express, and even feel, the wish that their country, or their part of it, should become a British Dominion, or a

Republic of the Soviet Union. Bavarians will denounce Prussians. Saxons, Silesians, Rhinelanders the rest. Few Germans, indeed, will profess any loyalty to Hitler or the Nazi faith; and, indeed, few at that time will have any. No nation in the world will have better cause to revile Hitler than the Germans; for of all the nations he will have laid low, he will have laid the German nation lowest. Thousands of Germans will wish only to leave their country, to forget it and its traditions for ever, and to emigrate to Australia or the Argentine, to China or Peru. There will probably be a strong religious revival: and there will be devotees, too, for creeds that never were German, like pacifism, or that have long ceased to have any real meaning in Germany, like Monarchy. One sect we are unlikely to find. If Germans become anarchists, something will really have happened.

2. We shall be wise not to pay too much attention to these transient symptoms. They will be symptoms of a disease, but not, probably, of a fatal one. Yet, this disease will inflict, while it lasts, almost unparalleled sufferings on the patient, and it will last some time. The reactions outlined above will have a common cause: the desire of Germans to escape from, to alleviate or to forget their pain.

3. This pain will result from the collapse of the standard of life. It will be the simple physical pain of acute need. Rations, low for more than five years, will certainly get much lower. Houses will be harder to come by than in any civilised country ever before. Clothes will be threadbare and irreplaceable. Fuel will be scarce. Transport will be chaotic. Personal property of every kind will have worn out or have disintegrated in the destruction of cities. Raw materials will be lacking, and manufactured goods for civil consumption will therefore be short. Employment may be intermittent, and its real reward will be small. Vitality, in a country which may well have suffered greater proportionate war casualties than any Great Power in any previous war, will be low. And to war casualties may be added those removed to the 'Siberian Captivity', which the Germans already so much dread.

4. This will be the crisis which will face individual Germans. In contemplation of it they may, for a long time, overlook the more

permanent injuries the war will have inflicted on their country. The German army may have been abolished and German heavy industry destroyed or curtailed; but German towns will be no more and no less in ruins for that. Germany may have been truncated or dismembered, but the same bread queue will stand before the same shop in the same German town. If Germany loses all territory east of the Oder, and if all Germans from such territory and from the Sudetenland are transferred back to Germany, then for every sixty Germans there were in the queue before there will now be ten more; but for a time the sixty may well hate the intruding transferees more than the act of transfer.

5. A soldier who loses a leg suffers from shock; he craves for hot tea, a cigarette and warm blankets. Only when he feels better does he begin to miss his leg. Germany after this war will suffer from national shock, and will search for palliatives of many kinds. When she begins to recover – as no doubt, some way behind the rest of the world, she will – she will begin to miss what she has lost. It is her reaction in this stage, rather than the acute symptoms of her prostration, that we should seek now to forecast and to study.

6. One symptom of the early stage should, however, be considered: regional feelings of aversion on the part of one set of Germans for another, and the 'separatist' movements to which they may give rise. Local feelings always have been, and still are, strong in Germany. Bavarians, on the whole, really do dislike Prussians – a good deal more than, say, Scots dislike Englishmen. But Bavarians do not, and in the long run will not, desire to cease being German citizens any more than Scots desire to cease being British subjects. The accentuation of such feelings in the post-defeat period, and the 'separatist' movements they may give rise to, will have two causes. First, the search for scapegoats, of which no doubt Germans will discover plenty; second, the desire of a regionally defined number of Germans to ingratiate themselves with the victors, and thereby to secure advantages for their region over other parts of Germany. But the history of separatist movements after the last war, both in the Rhineland and Bavaria, suggests it is unlikely that they will become, still less remain, strong after this war. Far fewer Germans exist now than in 1918 to whom

Baden, Saxony or even Prussia mean, or could be made to mean, anything comparable to what Germany has meant. Particularist feelings will be genuine enough, perhaps, to produce lasting support for a certain measure of decentralisation and local autonomy, which might be of some limited advantage to us: but not genuine enough to welcome real independence and exclusion from the rest of Germany. These feelings will vary in intensity with the intensity of the moral and economic crisis of Germany. As that crisis diminishes, so will particularist feelings.

7. When Germany begins to recover her breath, various factors will help to form the climate of German opinion. There will be factors of tradition and history: factors of recent experience – the experience of Nazism, the experience of war and defeat, and the experience of the settlement – whatever it be – imposed upon Germany. There will be such special factors as the existence in Germany of almost a generation – all Germans, more or less, born between 1910 and 1930 – which National Socialism has benighted and depraved. All these factors must be considered. But there will be one special factor, which did not exist in 1918, with which an intelligent German should in the future reckon, and on which we may base some hope.

8. After this war Germany will find that she has ceased, for the first time since 1870, to be potentially the strongest military power on the Continent of Europe. For 75 years she held that position, and in the last 30 of those years threw away, by repeated and extraordinary folly, the great advantages she had already derived and might have continued to derive from it. Already before this war the Nazis guessed that this position might be slipping away from them. That is the 'geo-political' justification for their attack on Russia; they hoped to strike Russia down before the balance tipped in her favour. They failed, and the balance has changed. Symptoms of the change are the reasonable estimates that German population will not increase after 1955, whereas Russian population will continue to increase rapidly till well on into the next century; and that by 1970 there will be, for every male German aged 20 to 34, four male Russians of similar age.

9. It must, of course, be realised that a similar decline in population, and therefore (neglecting for the moment other factors) in potential military power, will affect other countries of Western Europe. But the change in Germany's status in relation to that of Russia is likely to be sufficiently evident for one great fact to penetrate deeply and permanently into the German consciousness: that Germany will never again be able to challenge the whole world alone. Yet the deepest realisation of this fact will not be enough, by itself, to keep Germany out of mischief. If it were, we might be able to relax our vigilance. But even if Germany alone be unable again to challenge the world, she could yet challenge it with a powerful partner or combination of partners. This may change the character of the alliances she will seek, or even her sincerity in upholding them. She will want, perhaps, genuine partners, not mere jackals of opportunity. But this need not diminish her influence. Indeed, her diplomatic, as opposed to her military, influence may actually be increased. For if she ceases in European politics to be the factor of decision, she may become the main factor of equilibrium; thus acquiring opportunities of manoeuvre which she will know how to exploit. Germany's position in Europe after this war will perhaps be comparable – when she has recovered from the crisis of defeat – to that of this country at the beginning of this century, when we woke up to the fact that we needed allies, and proceeded to find them in Japan and in France. That we had not then reached the end of our power and success is sufficiently shown by the fact that we have since been among the victors in two world wars.

10. This train of thought leads straight to a critical question: will Germany seek to turn her back on the West and link her fortunes with the East? Before attempting to answer this, it will be better to continue the examination of the various psychological factors referred to above, which will themselves be of considerable importance in determining Germany's own answer to this question.

11. What impression will the colossal experience of this war leave on the mind of the German people, and what lessons will they draw from it? No doubt, when it is over and lost, the first reaction will be: Never again. But undoubtedly war is the logical, even if

sometimes undesired, expression of certain deep and hitherto abiding instincts and habits of the German people; and it would be rash to assume that even a second defeat in less than thirty years will by itself change those instincts and those habits. In particular it is dangerous to believe that the mere fact that this war has entailed unprecedented destruction in Germany, and savage fighting on German soil, will by itself make it unlikely that Germany will ever venture to indulge in war again. To be sure, some lively recollections will remain in the minds of individual Germans, and what they have suffered at home will make them dread war more. But unless as a people they become less docile, and therefore less slavishly subordinate to the power of their State; unless as individuals they become more individualistic, more responsible, more rebellious, and therefore less prone to see in order and discipline the proper conduct of life; then their mere passive preference for peace rather than war need not inhibit the policy of the German State. It did not in 1939. Their leaders wanted war, and they followed their leaders. If once again their leaders want war – which means if they see a good chance of waging war with success – then the whole experience of this war, the destruction in Germany of so many towns and homes and lives, may indeed make the average German march off once more with a heavier and more foreboding heart, but not less fast or far.

12. Moreover, future German recollections of this war will not all be tinged with defeat and disaster. Just as vividly they will remember how near they came to victory. They will remember the battles they won, the countries they struck down, the heroes who led them in success or perished in the hour of seeming triumph. The comradeship of an army, even a defeated and disbanded one, becomes when recollected in tranquillity a potent political factor. Those who take part in great campaigns, and survive them, remember them more rosily as they grow more remote; and this may prove as true for civilian battlefields – Coventry or Essen, London or Berlin – as of military ones. Nothing will stop the Germans from believing they had the finest army in the world, and succumbed only to superiority in numbers and material. Nothing will stop them taking pride in their accomplishments in a pursuit at which they so manifestly excel. Nothing, finally, will

stop them wishing to re-create armed forces when they have been deprived of them. This is the chief argument for not allowing them to do so; it is an argument against supposing that defeat can by itself eradicate German militarism. The lesson we must try to teach the Germans is not that war does not pay, or that war is futile or ignoble. The lesson must rather be that we can never pay *them*. We must so condition the evolution of Germany that the claws of militarism become rudimentary, and finally drop off. We must leave them no alternative to peace. Then, by necessity, they may become as peaceful as the Swiss. And let us remember that if there were 70,000,000 Swiss they might not be so peaceful after all.

13. Four factors lie at the root of German militarism. The first is history, and that we cannot change. Germany became great by force of arms, and will always suspect that she might repeat the process. The second is opportunity. In 1864, 1866 and 1870 Germany had the opportunity to profit by war; in 1914 and 1939 she thought she had. This, the most important factor of all, can be changed: Germany must be given no reason to hope she will ever have such an opportunity again. The third is discipline, by which is meant the instinct to organise and to obey, to exercise and to submit to authority. This we cannot, and events probably will not, much change. In Germany this instinct is carried to excess; and the reactions to defeat will certainly in the short run, and possibly even permanently, diminish its force. But it is not in itself a pernicious instinct; and it is of great value in other fields than war. In the case of Germany it is made pernicious by the fourth factor. This is that specifically German quality, so hard to define, so impossible to overlook, to analyse which so many books have been written. It is the highest common factor, and too high at that, of centuries of German poetry and philosophy: the dark, ecstatic and irrational element in German thought and conduct. Nothing is more rational than discipline: but nothing more irrational, by Western standards, than the German conception that the highest freedom can reside in subjection to it. It is this fatal idealism that has led in Germany to the eclipse of the individual and the cult of the community, to the aberrations of racial superiority and leader-worship, to the cult of brutality as

necessary to the complete denial of the value of the human personality, a denial on which this idealism insists. It is this idealism which gives to German militarism its monstrous quality, and has made the Nazi abroad the missionary of a daemonic cult. Will defeat change this? There is a chance that it may. The terrible, sobering effort of reconstruction, adjustment and atonement will purge away much of the infection; and it may be that, in the antiseptic atmosphere of prolonged national impotence, the canker will wither away. But we cannot be sure.

14. The experience of National Socialism may prove to have been more salutary to Germany than the experience of war and defeat. National Socialism will end in colossal failure. Here, again, it is possible that Germans will remember the nearness of success rather than the eventual disaster. But it is less likely than in the case of militarism. They will attribute such success as they had more to their natural qualities as Germans than to the superficial (as they will regard them) attributes of National Socialism, and indeed, in these attributes, and the leaders who incarnated them, will be found one of the most popular scapegoats for defeat. The legend of Hitler's genius will be hard put to it to survive intact the proofs of his military incapacity, which, when once he is out of the way, most Germans, and first of all the surviving military leaders, will be at pains to underline. This is fortunate for us, as a dead Hitler, without this handicap, might prove a powerful idol in years to come. As it is, there is probably no good reason for the more extreme fears sometimes expressed that the Nazi system as such will prove ineradicable in Germany, or that the legend of its leaders will keep alive or rekindle its doctrines. National Socialism will suffer, in German eyes, from the supreme demerit of having failed. Its end will bring to almost all Germans relief from certain restrictions or obligations that they have disliked. The immediate reaction against its principles, its methods and its personalities will be violent, and may become more so as Germans learn more than many of them now know about its real nature. National Socialism has been no more than a special form of organisation of the instincts, and capacities will remain largely what they are. But there is little reason to fear that National Socialism itself will revive; and some reason to hope that the experience of it will

have taught the Germans a few lessons which they will not forget. It would be superficial to regard Hitlerism as likely to remain a menace of the same order as German nationalism and German militarism. These two evils may unite again under a new totalitarian cloak; but it is not likely to be one of National Socialist cut.

15. To this analysis two important qualifications must, however, be made. The first concerns the 'lost generation', brought up to know no ideals and no career save those offered, no facts and no theories save those permitted by National Socialism. Some even of these, maybe, will yet contrive to work their passage home to more normal ways of living. But many will no more be able to live out of the atmosphere of National Socialism than a snail can out of its shell. Were there but few of them, policemen and psychiatrists might suffice to solve the problem: but there will be many. It is vain to hope that men such as the worst of these can be 're-educated'. Only drastic and severe remedies, such as prolonged internment or deportation or long labour service outside Germany in the reconstruction of devastated countries hold out any hope of working them out of Germany's system. In her convalescence Germany, after injection with other ideas, may be immune from their contagion: but both Germany and Europe will need protection from their violence.

16. The second qualification is of more importance. To say that National Socialism is unlikely to remain, or become again, a popular creed in Germany does not mean that Germany is likely to become democratic. Germany will once again have the choice – or so it might seem – between the ideals of the West and of the East, between an individualist and a collectivist system. Unfortunately, there can be little doubt what her choice will be. Many German individuals, and perhaps even the majority in some districts of Germany – Baden, the Rhineland, the Hanseatic cities – may understand and prefer the Western tradition of individual freedom and the concept of the State as the servant, not the master, of its citizen. But even they have long regarded this system with nostalgia, as something unobtainable, impracticable and essentially unsuited to Germany, rather than with passion, as something to be fought for, acquired and jealously preserved. To the

great majority of Germans, on the other hand, personal liberty, the active rule of the majority, even the rule of law, have long seemed things not perhaps undesirable, but not important when weighed against the claims of the State to impose discipline, organisation and efficiency for its own supreme ends. In the last resort, Germans are not interested in politics. They do not think of the action of the State as being a reflection of their own wills. They prefer that it should circumscribe and define the limits within which their individual wills may act. They are therefore, in the political sense, irresponsible: they reject the burden and duty of choice. Thus there can be no hope for liberalism in Germany. Liberals cannot force people – not even to be free. But the German mass is determined to be forced. It insists on abdication. And it will abdicate to the first party that presents it with an inviting straitjacket. It is probably vain to hope that National Socialism will have stimulated contrary desires by thwarting them. It will rather have extinguished them altogether. We shall not find the individual reacting against the community; on the contrary, we shall find that Germans cut adrift and turned into individuals by the collapse of one system, will look for another. They will seek again the stability of a new community, the warmth of immersion in a new mass. Whether the plunge goes left or right will matter, in the long run, comparatively little to us. None of the typically German patterns of thought and behaviour discussed above, which have flourished in a Fascist Germany, need be inhibited, or even much altered, in a Communist one. But unless the West has more to offer Germany than Germans at present believe, we must be prepared to find that National Socialism has confirmed and completed the trend of centuries, and that Germany is lost, for good and all, to the Western world.

17. An attempt may now be made to answer the question: would Germany, in another war crisis, be found on the side of the East or the West? Circumstances can alter any case. But if German inclinations and calculations are to determine the matter, then the answer must be as pessimistic as most of the other conclusions so far arrived at in this paper. Germany will be found on the side of the East, because her political and social ideas and instincts will align her with the East rather than the West. And this conclusion

on grounds of psychology is reinforced by two practical reasons, of even greater importance, why Germany should look East rather than West. First, she will never again wish to try conclusions with Russia: those who oppress the weak side with the strong. Second, Russia will, if she so chooses, be in a position, and the West will not, to restore to Germany what she will most passionately long to recover: the territory she is about to lose to Poland.

18. The mere resentment of defeat and disarmament, quite apart from the final political, economic and territorial settlement imposed upon her, will be enough no doubt to inflame nationalist and militarist feelings in Germany. But Germans do understand that lost wars involve losses; and they might accept and become resigned to a settlement which imposed on them heavy servitudes, including territorial losses up to a certain point. It is, however, a fact simple and unoriginal but inescapable, that Germany's mental reaction to defeat will be determined, in the long run, not by the mere fact of defeat, but by the settlement it leads to. It will be determined most of all by the territorial settlement, and by such possible accompanying burdens as the wholesale transfer of populations from ceded areas, which would spread throughout the remainder of Germany the unappeasable determination of irredentism and the bitterness of the dispossessed. To exacerbate Germany's feelings of nationalism and militarism by inflicting on her very extensive territorial losses, which she will regard as unjust and intolerable and to which she will never become resigned, would gravely diminish any hope there may be that Germany might eventually become reconciled to the settlement of Europe, and co-operate in its maintenance.

19. The more it is outraged, the greater is the risk that the ideal of militant Germany will revive. It is an ideal dangerous to ourselves. If, beyond a certain necessary point, we can let it alone, this dangerous ideal may die or be displaced. To displace it a new ideal will be needed, an alternative and harmless ideal. It must be one which can attract and employ the great capacities and the great skill of the German people; and it must give them a hope of satisfying that odd desire by which they have always been haunted – the desire to be respected, admired and loved by the rest of the world. We must, if possible, find an ideal that exists

already in Germany's traditions: and one such can be found. It is the idea of social and intellectual progress. Germany must be encouraged to aim at being a super-Sweden, cleaner, better planned and healthier than any State ever was before, with better social, medical and educational services and a higher standard of living than any State ever had. It is not a bad programme for a defeated country; but even in such a programme there are dangers. We must keep an eye on her philosophy, and still more, war being what it has become, on her science. But the alternative to some such sublimating alternative ideal is only the old pernicious one, and can lead only to the old pernicious trouble: it is the ideal of the German people and the German nation. The excessive mutilation of Germany by truncation, or her abolition by dismemberment, will lead only to the re-establishment of the ideal of the German Reich. If we are confident that we shall retain the means and the will to resist its dangers, then let us by all means risk the re-establishment of this ideal. But not otherwise.

20. And if we are to place before Germany the ideal of the social state, of the rising standard of life, then we should refrain, where possible, even in the earliest days of peace, from action which will make that ideal seem impossibly far off. Unemployment in Germany may prove as deadly to Europe as national pride. National Socialism found jobs for all; and whatever else the Germans may forget about it, they will not forget that. The German people have great energy and great skill. If at first these cannot be employed to their own profit, at least they should be employed to the general profit of Europe.

21. If this analysis has any lesson for us, it is perhaps that we should not hasten, in the artificial atmosphere and depression of a defeated country, to impose servitudes, political or economic, that may later promote the rebirth of German militarism, at a time when we may be less disposed and perhaps less able to resist it. We should concentrate on what is necessary for our own security, remembering that the purpose of the peace, as of the war, is not to punish the Germans but to secure our own safety and advantage. We should also see to it that certain lessons are learnt by the Germans. They are: that Germany can never again challenge the world alone; that the other Powers will never permit her

to join one of them in challenging the rest; and therefore that she must cease to mourn for her military past, or hope to recreate it, and see her future instead in terms of a new and different conception.

Foreign Office, 2 January, 1945

NOTES ON THE MENTALITY OF THE GERMAN OFFICER[2]

Memorandum prepared by Brigadier Van Cutsem, Historical Research Control Commission (British Element) on mentality of German officers as experienced by officers formerly British Service Attachés in Berlin.

15 January 1945

1. The Influence of Tradition on the German Officer

(a) Perhaps we shall understand the German officer better if we trace the development of his curious mentality through earlier years. Now the great majority of officers with whom the Control Commission after 1918 dealt had been educated in a Royal Cadet College and had subsequently served in the Imperial Army. They had enjoyed all the great privileges, the prestige and high social standing of the Offizierkorps. They were steeped in two centuries of Prussian military tradition: they accepted the legends of Prussia (*preussischer Mythos*) and Sedan (*Mythos von Sedan*) as gilt-edged truths; the former proclaims Prussia's world mission, the latter the invincibility of the German Army.

In his book *Deutschland nach dem Kriege von 1866*, written about 1870, Freiheer [*sic*] von Ketteler, Bishop of Mainz, states: 'The term *Preussischer Mythos* or *Borussianismus* signifies a fixed idea concerning the vocation of Prussia, an abstruse conception of a Mission entrusted to Prussia, combined with the conviction that this Mission is a vital necessity and will be fulfilled as surely as a detached rock is compelled by gravity to roll down a steep slope.

To the adherents of *Borrossianismus* it is therefore inadmissible to oppose this mystical World Mission in the name of right or by appeal to history; it stands above every law. In executing it Prussia must be merciless.'

After the King of Prussia became German Kaiser in 1871, this Prussian Mission automatically became 'Germany's destined Mission to impose her will on Europe and dominate the world'. Mendacity and breach of faith in dealing with neighbouring States and other peoples were considered justified and wholly approved as means to that end. The Offizierkorps of the Kaiserreich were fanatically devoted to duty; they worshipped military efficiency and were interested in naught else. The recognised only the person of the Monarch as their supreme Commander 'by the grace of God', and did not consider themselves to be just servants of the nation. Later, under the mischievous influence of Wilhelm II, the spirit of the Offizierkorps deteriorated in many respects: boastfulness, cocksureness and arrogance came to the fore. Though lipservice was still paid to Christian ethics, they were never allowed to interfere with the policy and welfare of the Army. The collective attitude of the Military towards Britain in those days was one of jealousy and envy of her power and prestige: it was intolerable that these decadent mercenary British should be counted the leading Germanic people.

The crisis of 1918 was far-reaching. The Offizierkorps lost their Monarch and their privileged position; their numbers were severely cut down. Defeat had cast reflections on their own military efficiency. The caste felt humiliated and embittered, but quickly concentrated all efforts towards one aim, a war of revenge, an end which justified any means. Their motives were more rooted in the interests of their caste than inspired by pure patriotism.

(b) There is one particularly tiresome trait which most Prussians have inherited from their mixed Germanic and Slav ancestry, viz: a certain Germanic faculty for hard thinking, offset by a strong Slav tendency to believe in fanciful flights of imagination. The result is that even today a Prusso-German officer will often stubbornly pursue some new theory to an absurd or quite inhuman conclusion, and solemnly adhere to it; many are thus irritatingly dogmatic and deficient in their sense of proportion. The officers of the General Staff are, however, usually highly intelligent men with wide vision and balanced minds.

2. German Officers and the Treaty of Versailles

About 1931 when the Germans were making a serious bid to bring about the Anschluss with Austria and were putting out a lot of very heated propaganda on the subject, I happened to be invited to a dinner party by Colonel Fischer, who was then the German D.M.I. (Chef der Fremden-Abteilung). While we were having a drink before dinner I started to chaff Fischer mildly about the propaganda on the subject, which I had been reading in the German press, and remarked to him that I thought it very stupid of the Germans to try and break down an important provision of the Versailles Treaty in such a blatant way. Colonel Fischer drew himself up, looked at me with intense scorn and said, 'We are tired of being treated like a Nigger State and we shall soon tear up your Versailles Treaty'.

Another incident happened in March 1935 when I was staying in Berlin with my successor. He had asked several of my old German acquaintances to meet me at dinner, including General von Blomberg, who was then Chef der Heeresleitung. After dinner we happened to be discussing the Italian attempts to browbeat the Abyssinians. Bomberg said to me, 'This is a particularly interesting moment for us, and we are watching the situation very closely; last year you British let the Japanese get away with their *fait accompli* in Manchuria; this year if you are equally weak about the Italians and Abyssinia, we Germans will know exactly where we are, and we shall be able to do just what we like in Central Europe and in tearing up the Versailles Treaty.'

On the following day I went round to the Reichswehrministerium to call on my old friend Reichenau, who had just been promoted Major-General and, I think, occupied the position either equivalent to a D.M.O. or D.S.D. under Blomberg. While we were having a talk, Reichenau suddenly said to me, 'By the way, would you like to go down to Wünsdorf and see our new Tank Regiment?' I was somewhat astonished and said, 'But surely you aren't allowed to have any tanks by the Treaty; since when have you had tanks?' Reichenau replied, 'Of course you know we have had a Tank Regiment for quite a long time, but anyway tomorrow you will be able to read all about it in the newspapers'. Next day the German Government announced that it had thrown off the military clauses of the Versailles Treaty and was introducing conscription, and had raised a force of 36 Divisions, equipped with tanks, heavy artillery and aircraft...

4. The German Officer's Conception of Honour

(a) The German word 'Ehre', by which the dictionaries translate our word 'Honour', really means 'Face'. A British officer about to leave Germany asked a German colonel of the General Staff to a goodbye dinner. They were personal friends and the invitation was accepted. At the last moment the German colonel's secretary telephoned he had lumbago and could not come. He admitted afterwards his real reason was annoyance at a reply in the House of Commons, which stated an arrangement had been made at a German request, when it would have been more accurate to say 'by mutual request'. German 'face' had suffered. The German officer's honour is thus objective, i.e. it suffers by other people's actions...

(b) The outstanding characteristic of the German officer is that by virtue of the fact that he is an officer he enjoys a marked prestige in Germany. He expects and receives certain privileges that are denied to the ordinary civilian. Perhaps as a result of this the German officer will tell any lie and expects to get away with it. He seems to think that as an officer and a gentleman his word cannot possibly be questioned, but he is not in the least ashamed if he is found out. In about 1933 the British Air Attaché in Berlin was given some information by a German officer concerning the steps that Germany was taking to build up an air force in contravention of the terms of the Versailles Treaty. A report was sent to the Air Ministry and a complaint was in due course lodged with the Ministry of Foreign Affairs in Berlin which disclosed the name of the informant. The latter and the Air Attaché were summoned to appear before Goering, when the informant flatly denied having said anything of the sort. This was told to a British officer by the informant, who was not in the least ashamed to confess that he had lied.

Conversely the German officer expects to be lied to. One day when on a visit to Cranwell, Milch, who was then virtual chief of the German Air Force, asked some question about the Royal Air Force. It was a matter of slight importance and the British accompanying officer picked up the Air Force List from the table and gave him the answers from it. Milch looked at Wenninger, the German Attaché in London, gave a wry smile and turned back to the British officer. They obviously thought that he had devised rather a clumsy way of giving false information.

5. The Present Day German Officer

(a) The younger German officer today is likely to be profoundly influenced by the National-Socialist German Labour Party teaching he received before joining the Army. This will make him more human with like-minded patriotic Aryan Germans, but will not change those of his characteristics which are objectionable from the control point of view. The old blind patriotism is if anything intensified. A standard grace before dinner at the compulsory premilitary Labour Service (RAD) camps was, 'Everything for Germany, that is our religion'. What is virtuous if done by a German and good for Germany, causes pained surprise and horror if done by a foreigner and prejudicial to German interests.

(b) One drill is to keep certain of their own officers ill-informed, so that these can place hand on heart and swear an untrue fact that they believe true. Given an order by his own superior, the German's conscience has a clearance certificate and does not function.

(c) As to the new types of obstruction which our control officers will presently have to handle, I hesitate to express any opinion. I cannot draw reliable conclusions from my close personal associations with Goering, Milch, and other members of the Wehrmacht and Nazi Party up to 1938/39, because the whole political situation in Germany will have changed so much. Maybe our people will encounter on the surface a layer of smooth-tongued stooges and intriguers, but the core beneath is certain to prove of much coarser grain, more ferociously fanatic and more contemptuous of any kind of moral restraint than was the case when we were up against them twenty years ago. Nevertheless, there will be some fierce factional splits amongst them, and in time, plenty of denouncers; this, combined with the fact that the Germans as liars are clumsy and transparent (far inferior to the Latins), may assist the task of our control officers.

THE GERMAN CHARACTER[3]

This account can only aim at a generalisation and it must be read accordingly, taking into account the limitations of such treatment. This applies particularly in the case of Germans owing to the complexity of the German character.... Therefore all the characteristics mentioned are unlikely to be encountered in any one individual; some may be contradicted; others not mentioned will be present. All that can be attempted is to show a cross-section, neither of the leaders nor the extreme fanatics, but of the *average* German.

It must be affirmed that the Germans are not divided into two classes, good and bad Germans: there are only good and bad elements in the German character, the latter of which generally predominate. But it may be said with a good deal of truth that the Germans can be divided into two other classes, namely the leaders who plot and plan, and the led who blindly follow, and that these two are equally dangerous and make up the great majority of all Germans.

Complexity

The Germans are easily the most mixed race in Europe, contrary to the ignorant and perverse Nazi theories of membership of a single Aryan master race; for no race is a master race and the Aryan race has never existed. Though subject throughout her history to Western and Eastern influences, Germany stands geographically in the middle. Broadly speaking she has adopted neither a Western nor an Eastern civilization or culture, but something peculiarly her own, known as 'Kultur', not civilization nor yet culture as others understand them: an embodiment of those ideals, at one time characterized as Prussian, but at present shared by Germans as a whole.

The German character is therefore complex, full of paradox most difficult to understand by a people like the British whose character is simpler and who have developed by a more natural and gradual process. In fact German unity is a very recent and artificial growth and in times of crisis the underlying fundamental disunity emerges on the surface. Again, while the Germans economically, technically and in matters of organisation are in the forefront, politically they are among the most backward. The German character is also in many respects primitive; this is emphasized by the regard for historical tradition, in the forms of admiration of the Middle Ages and of the cruelties, intolerances and occultism that marked the dark period, and of the earlier brutal and savage Teutonic tribes. The more extreme, but numbering prominent men among them, indeed openly exult in being 'modern barbarians'.

Extremist Tendencies

It has been remarked that 'in Germany everything is carried to extremes'. Nazism itself is just an extreme manifestation of the German character. The Germans stress fanatical will-power, work and sacrifice, and they exalt death rather than life, all of which causes them to become subject to great strain, resulting in those familiar traits of lack of spontaneity, heaviness, morbid introspection, unhappiness, and a fatalistic sense of ultimate doom, which in certain conditions culminate in breakdowns and mania, and account for the high suicide rate. This should be contrasted with the immense hidden reserves of more indolent people like the British. Such over-driving causes the formation of a hard brittle exterior and a holding out till the bitter end, only to be followed by sudden and complete collapse entailing extreme demoralisation. Among the die-hard fanatics collapse produces differing reactions – hysteria, running amok, killings and destruction of others or self. In general, there will appear all the constituent elements of chaos.

Double Personality

Double personality or mental split is a remarkable side of the German character. It arises from various causes: an inferiority complex due in part to Germany's late start as a nation, a guilt complex resulting from misdeeds, and at the same time an awareness of great gifts and talents. This last is coupled with the feeling that despite great achievements in literature, science, the arts and industry, Germany has been denied her 'place in the sun' and has had her birthright filched by altogether less deserving nations who have conspired to prevent her from reaching those standards of living and well-being which should be hers. So we find the attitude that Germany is 'poor', though her resources in fact transcend those of the rest of Europe.

Duality produces divided feelings towards others: love and hate, admiration and jealousy or envy; submissiveness and the wish to dominate. Another aspect of this duality is the prevalence of two standards; there may be one standard of personal conduct, but there will be an entirely different kind in official conduct or in matters where the imagined rights of Germany are concerned. This outlook is exemplified again in the attitude to war as a continuous natural state, whereas peace is regarded as the brief enjoyment of power.

Adaptability

Double personality in turn causes the emergence of alternate ascendancies, such as the assertion of superiority and arrogance, and humility and fawning. These ascendancies evince themselves under contrasting conditions, victory or defeat, but it must be emphasized that they are capable of rapid reversal should anything occur to lead the Germans to believe that the state of affairs which has given rise to one particular ascendancy is showing signs of a change. Thus in defeat there will be little or no manifestation of racial pride among the great majority and this attitude is likely now to be more pronounced than ever, especially among the young, owing to the boomerang effect of Nazi propaganda which has succeeded to a large extent in 'denationalising' them.

This adaptability moreover enables almost automatic assumption of the outward attitude considered most likely to fit the circumstances, hence the adroitness of the individual German in efforts to divide his conquerors. It will show itself in endeavours to ingratiate himself with them by informing against other Germans, a further example of the fundamental disunity referred to above.

Subjectivity

The Germans, particularly under the Nazis, have been taught to disdain reason and to be guided by emotion; they are in fact a highly emotional people. In this connection it is no accident that they have excelled in that most emotional of all arts, music. This subjectivity and emotionalism partly explain those fantastic notions, most marked among the younger generation of Nazis, for instance their extraordinary vehemence and determination to carry through their self-imposed mission to conquer and rule other races, combined with an apparently sincere astonishment at the base ingratitude of the others who decline to recognise the benefits being conferred upon them.

Reason cannot argue with emotion and the German therefore readily accepts the legend, with its emotional appeal, and disregards the sober truth. Subjectivity shows itself again in inability to see any other point of view but the German and in the general belief that what it is right for Germany to do is not at all right for others to do. A natural consequence of subjectivity is a lack of balance and tenacity in convictions; thus what is thought and said at one moment in all sincerity (though more or less with subconscious reservations), may be the absolute opposite of what is similarly thought and said at a later moment, and without awareness of any inconsistency.

The general command or prohibition, or the slogan, to which the German loves to submit his own will, acts directly on his emotion, and accounts for his displaying the same fanaticism in blindly following his leader as in pitilessly enforcing sanctions against others.

Subjectivity is also one of the main reasons for German self-pity and skill in organising sympathy for themselves, combined with a complete absence of German sympathy for their victims or repentance for their acts. Subjectivity and the discouragement of independent thought supply; moreover, the reasons for the average German being so gullible and so fruitful a target for propaganda. Other consequences of subjectivity are intolerance, the inability to compromise, and the tendency to regard any suggestion for concession on the German side as an insult to German 'honour'.

Cult of False Values

This is accounted for by the widely different outlook on the individual and his position in life, as opposed to that of Western philosophy. The means is confused with the end and is sufficient in itself. The individual exists for the State (or Party); the latter can therefore only exist for itself and its sole object must be to organise and to keep on organising. Hence the insistence on the dynamic and on change for the sake of change. All is restlessness, nothing static; the Nazi Party itself is a 'movement'. Where there is a conscious end, then it justifies the means; what is good for Germany brooks neither challenge nor opposition. There can thus be no concept of abstract or absolute ethical values, such as truth, justice, honesty, and their opposites, but only what is right or wrong for Germany. Consequently deceit, lying, crime are all perfectly legitimate in the cause of Germany.

So warped a moral code naturally leads to the conclusion that the way Germans do anything must automatically be the best and that the systems or methods of others are out-moded, inferior and to be despised. The German has accordingly the urge to dominate, with or without war. Negotiating a contract or State Treaty is regarded as a battle, in which there can only be victor and vanquished. The agreement has no binding force, but holds good merely so long as it serves the Germans or Germany's interest. War is regarded as something sublime and of an intrinsic grandeur; all is fair in war; in waging war no law of humanity is recognised, in fact the more brutal the behaviour the more humane the war, since it will end sooner in (German) victory. Moreover 'might' is 'right' and 'he who has the greater might has the greater right'. These are not the ravings of some lunatic, but the serious utterances of foremost statesmen and writers, which have been acclaimed with avidity and enthusiasm by the German masses.

The glorification of war and its anticipated benefits is also a symptom of the German worship of success. This general materialistic outlook, which is one of the worst of the German false cults, is partly due to the feverish over-industrialization of Germany since 1870, which has resulted in a too sudden prosperity and has assigned exaggerated importance to material, as opposed to moral, welfare. One consequence of all this wrongheadedness is the reliance on and parrotlike repetition of slogans, shibboleths and catch-words, to replace real convictions. The lack of these and of firm moral tenets produces a vacuum or negation, when the falseness of such cults is shown up through disaster.

Sense of Inferiority

The Germans have a deep-seated inferiority complex, partly caused by grievances, such as the late emergence of Germany as a nation. But it is primarily due to that submission to forceful authority which results in the need to compensate the inner doubt by a search for status and an endeavour to over-valuate self by outward expression. It thus betrays itself by a reverse external attitude of superiority (*Herrenvolk*) and arrogance, desire to enhance prestige by ranks and titles, resentment and readiness to look for insults. It also includes a feeling of individual loneliness, of isolation from other nations, and of disunity and antipathy among Germans themselves. Hence the tendency to seek strength, cohesion and solidarity by herding together and sinking the individual in the mass. The love of parades, pageantry, colours, uniforms and emblems and other outward signs of an association or community are all manifestations of this trend. At the same time the ability to identify himself completely with some organisation, whether Wehrmacht, SS or other, is an element making for great strength and accounts for the outstanding tenacity of the German when a member of a group.

Regard for Authority

The respect for authority is almost universal and is typified in the German love of order. But whilst physical bravery is general, moral courage is uncommon. It is for these reasons that revolutionary movements are very rare in German history, and that blind obedience is not only demanded but willingly offered. Such obedience relieves the German from responsibility for any crime committed in pursuance of an order – his conscience is by-passed. Blind obedience and unswerving loyalty to an appointed or a chosen leader has a psychological counterpart which is no less dangerous. Once the German has laid down a principle, framed a law or a code of conduct – usually a prohibition – his acceptance is absolute and his implementation totalitarian. Impelled by this categoric 'thou shalt' or 'thou shalt not', he imposes sanctions of excessive severity and vindictiveness, and shrinks from no degree of brutality in their execution. His inhuman treatment of hostages is merely one example.

In the same authoritarian trend is the awe of an expert – the professor, the technician, and above all the military expert, according to his rank. Although a German is taught to think within his own particular sphere, outside it what authority lays down must be right – the word of the expert is gospel. It has indeed been aptly remarked that 'the German is expert rather than wise'. This is very true, for if he were wise he could not accept without question those theories, so absurd to others, in which he dogmatically believes; and, if not expert, the Germans could not through their efficiency, thoroughness and industry have raised Germany to be by far the strongest power in Europe.

Authority connotes force, and force is thus also worshipped. At the same time the leader, as the personification of authority, is also looked upon as the good father. Accordingly the follower is bound to the leader by both fear and love – an example of the mental split previously mentioned. But this binding obedience to authority has certain consequences. In the first place repressions, like the denial of the rights of the individual or of natural feelings not considered to be 'manly', produce pent-up resentment against authority which seeks relief in aggression, tyranny and sadistic treatment of others. This sadistic trait is not peculiar to the Nazis: the ordinary German, the husband and father, will derive pleasure in carrying out orders involving the infliction of torture and suffering. Yet in between he will take out the photo of his wife and children and slobber over it.

In the second place allegiance to authority is given in return for anticipated success and the material benefits flowing from it. Thus the failure of the leader and what he stands for cannot be condoned. Nothing is too bad for the fallen idol; he is turned against and held to blame for all Germany's misfortunes. In this way the individual German himself escapes moral responsibility by a simple process of finding a scapegoat and shifting the blame. Thus he says 'he was never a Nazi or "political"', but was 'forced to obey' and 'was lied to and betrayed'. He is deeply aggrieved, full of complaints, the innocent victim of the wiles of others. From this it is easy to reverse completely for himself the nature of the cause which he at one time so enthusiastically espoused – the conquest and subjection of others. It now becomes 'the war forced on Germany', forestalling of 'encirclement', or the championing of 'Europe' against 'Bolshevism'. By such process aggression in itself can never be deplored but only the *failure* of aggression through a lost war, for a lost war does not pay.

ANNOUNCEMENTS BY GERMAN LEADERS, 1–8 MAY 1945[4]

1. Hitler's Death: Dönitz's Statement

North German Home Service, 22:26 hrs, 1 May 1945

ANNOUNCER: The German wireless broadcasts grave and important news for the German people. [*Three rolls of drums.*] It is reported from the Führer's headquarters that our Führer, Adolf Hitler, fighting to the last breath against Bolshevism, fell for Germany this afternoon at his operational headquarters in the Reich Chancellery. On the 30th April he appointed Admiral of the Fleet Dönitz his successor. The Admiral of the Fleet and successor of the Führer speaks to the German people.

DÖNITZ: German men and women, soldiers of the German armed forces! Our Führer, Adolf Hitler, has fallen. In deepest sorrow and veneration the German people bows its head. At an early date he recognised the terrible danger of Bolshevism, and dedicated his existence to this struggle. At the end of this his struggle, of his unswerving and straight journey through life, stands his hero's death in the capital of the German Reich. His life has been one act of service to Germany. His activity in the fight against the Bolshevik storm flood was dedicated beyond this to Europe and the entire civilised world. The Führer has appointed me his successor. Fully conscious of the responsibility, I take over the leadership of the German people at this fateful hour.

It is my first task to save the German people from destruction by the advancing Bolshevik enemy. For this aim alone the military struggle continues. As far and so long as the achievement of this aim is impeded by the British and Americans we shall be forced to carry on our defensive fight against them too. In such conditions, however, the Anglo-Americans will be continuing the war not for their own peoples but solely for the spreading of Bolshevism in Europe. What the German people has achieved in battle and borne in the Homeland during the struggle of this war is unique in history. In the coming time of need and crisis for our people I shall endeavour to establish tolerable conditions of living for our women, men and children, so far as lies in my power.

For all this I need your help. Give me your confidence, for your road is also my road. Maintain order and discipline in town and country. Let everybody do his duty at his post. Only thus shall we mitigate the sufferings which the coming time will bring to each of us; only thus shall we be able to prevent a collapse. If we do all in our power, the Lord God will not forsake us after so much suffering and sacrifice. [*Deutschland über Alles* and *Horst-Wessel song.*]

2. Germany Bulwark against Bolshevism: Speech by Count Schwerin von Krosigk

North German Home Service, 21:00 hrs, 2 May 1945

German men and women! Admiral of the Fleet Dönitz, whom the Führer appointed as his successor, has charged me with the duties of Reich Foreign Minister. In Germany's hardest hour I address myself to the public. As yet the world still rings with the din of battle. German men are still falling in their last fight for the defence of the German Homeland. Over the roads of those parts of Germany which are not yet occupied rolls a stream of desperate, starving human beings, hunted by fighter-bombers, in flight to the west from unspeakable terror. In the east, the iron curtain is advancing even further, behind which the work of annihilation proceeds hidden from the eyes of the world.

At San Francisco they are discussing the organisation of a new world order which is to give mankind security from another war. The world knows that a third world war would mean not the doom of one nation but the end of mankind. The terrible weapons which did not come to be used in this war would come into effect in a third world war and bring death and destruction to the whole of mankind. Of all the people in the world, we Germans have experienced most strongly what even now war means in the destruction of all civilisation. Our towns are destroyed. Our cultural monuments in Dresden and Nürnberg, Köln, Bayreuth and other world-famous cities of the German cultural creation lie in ruins. Our cathedrals have become the victims of bombs. Hundreds of thousands of women and children have been struck down by the fury of war, while millions of German men and youths have fallen at the fronts. From the hearts of tormented wives and mothers there rises the prayer to heaven that the world may be preserved from the frightful terrors of another world war, but this prayer, strongest and most fervent among the German people. With us, all the European peoples, threatened by famine and Bolshevik terror, long for order which is to give this continent, ploughed up by the fury of war, a true and lasting peace and the possibility of a free and secure life.

But the more German territory in the east, which ought to form a basis for food supplies for the starving people in the west, falls into the hands of the Bolsheviks, the most speedily and terribly will famine sweep over Europe. Nurtured by this distress, Bolshevism flourishes. A Bolshevised Europe constitutes the first phase on the path towards a world revolution which the Soviets have been persistently pursuing for over twenty-five years. The achievement of this aim or a third world war are the unavoidable alternatives. Therefore we do not see in San Francisco the fulfilment of that for which mankind strives in its anxiety. We too believe that a world order will have to be established which not only prevents future wars, but also effects a timely elimination of potential centres from which a cause for war might arise. But such an order cannot merely be created by appointing the Red incendiarist one of the guardians of peace. Peace can be brought to the world only if the Bolshevik tidal wave does not flood Europe. In a heroic fight which knows no equal, Germany for four years, summoning her last ounce of strength, formed the bulwark of Europe and the entire world against the Red flood. She could have saved Europe from Bolshevism had her rear not been menaced.

As much as for external peace humanity longs for inward peace for the solution of the social problem which is burning in every country. This solution cannot be found in Bolshevism, but only in a just social order which respects the freedom and dignity of man. We believe honestly that we made a contribution towards solving this question when we showed that unemployment and crises can be overcome even under the most difficult economic conditions, and established within our orbit just and worthy working and living conditions for the workers, and thus deprived Bolshevism of the soil on which it can grow.

3. High Command's Surrender: Broadcast by Krosigk

The Times, 8 May 1945: 'Germany Has Succumbed'

Count Schwerin von Krosigk, the German Foreign Minister, broadcast the following announcement from Flensburg yesterday:

'German men and women, the high command of the armed forces has to-day at the order of Grand Admiral Dönitz, declared the unconditional surrender of all fighting German troops. As the leading Minister of the Reich Government which the Grand Admiral has appointed for dealing with war tasks, I turn at this tragic moment of our history to the German nation. After a heroic fight of almost six years of incomparable hardness, Germany has succumbed to the overwhelming power of her enemies. To continue the war would only mean senseless bloodshed and a futile disintegration.

'A Government which has feeling of responsibility for the future of its nation was compelled to act on the collapse of all physical and material forces and to demand of the enemy the cessation of hostilities. It was the noblest task of the Grand Admiral and of the Government supporting him, after the terrible sacrifices which the war demanded, to save in the last phase of the war the lives of a maximum number of fellow countrymen. That the war was not ended immediately, simultaneously in the west and in the east, is to be explained by this reason alone.

'In this gravest hour of the German nation and its Reich, we bow in deep reverence before the dead of this war. Their sacrifices place the highest obligations on us. Our sympathy goes out above all to the wounded, the bereaved, and to all on whom this struggle has inflicted blows.

No Illusions

'No one must be under any illusions about the severity of the terms to be imposed on the German people by our enemies. We must now face our fate squarely and unquestioningly. Nobody can be in any doubt that the future will be difficult for each one of us, and will exact sacrifices from us in every sphere of life. We must accept this burden, and stand loyally by the obligations we have undertaken. But we must not despair and fall into mute resignation. Once again we must set ourselves to stride along a path through the dark future. From the collapse of the past, let us preserve and save one thing, the unity of ideas of a national community which in the years of war have found their highest expression in the spirit of comradeship at the front and readiness to help one another in all the distress which has afflicted the homeland.

'In our nation justice shall be the supreme law and the guiding principle. We must also recognize law as the basis of all relations between the nations. We must recognize it and respect it from inner conviction. Respect for treaties will be as sacred as the aim of our nation to belong to the European family of nations, as a member of which we want to mobilize all human, moral, and material forces in order to heal the dreadful wounds which the war has caused. Then we may hope that the atmosphere of hatred which to-day surrounds Germany all over the world will give place to a spirit of reconciliation among the nations without which the world cannot recover.' — *Reuter*

Count Schwerin von Krosigk also said:
'Then we may hope that our freedom will be restored to us, without which no nation can lead a bearable and dignified existence. We wish to devote the future of our nation to the return of the inmost and best forces of German nature, which have given to the world imperishable works and values. We view with pride the heroic struggle of our people, and we shall combine with our pride in the heroic struggle of our people the will to contribute, as a member of western culture, honest, peaceful labour – a contribution which expresses the best traditions of our nation. May God not forsake us in our distress and bless us in our heavy task.'
— *British United Press*

4. Speech by Dönitz

Flensburg, 8 May 1945

German men and women: In my address on 1 May, in which I informed the German nation of the death of the Führer and of my appointment as his successor, I described it as my primary task to save the lives of German people. To attain this goal I ordered, during the night of 6 May, the High Command of the Wehrmacht to declare the unconditional surrender of all fighting forces in all theatres of war. On 8 May at 23:00, hostilities will cease. The soldiers of the German armed forces, who have proved their mettle in countless battles, will set out on the bitter road to captivity, thus making their last sacrifice for the lives of our women and children, for the future of our nation. We bow in reverence before the thousand-fold proven gallantry and sacrifice of our dead and prisoners.

I have promised the German people that I shall endeavour, in the coming times of distress, to provide tolerable living conditions for our gallant women, men and children, as far as this is within my power. I do not know whether I shall be able to help you in these hard days. We must face facts squarely. The foundations on which the German Reich was built have collapsed. The unity of State and party no longer exists. The party has left the scene of its activities. When Germany is occupied, control will be in the hands of the Occupying Powers. It rests with them whether or not

I and the Reich Government appointed by me will be able to function. If by my service in office I can be useful and of assistance to our Fatherland I shall remain in office until the will of the German people can find expression in the selection of a head of State or until the Occupying Powers render it impossible for me to continue in office. For I am bound to my difficult position only by my love for the fatherland and my duty. I shall not remain for an hour longer than, without regard to my own person, this can be reconciled with the dignity I owe the Reich, whose supreme representative I am.

We all have a hard road ahead of us. We must travel with the dignity, bravery and discipline which the memory of our fallen demands from us. We must travel it with the determination to work to the utmost of our capacity, without which we cannot create a basis for our life. We will travel it with unity and justice, without which we cannot overcome the distress of the coming time. We may travel it with the hope that our children may one day have a secure existence in a pacified Europe. I do not wish to lag behind you on this thorny path. If duty demands that I should remain in office, I will try to help you, as far as lies in my power. If duty demands that I should go, this step shall also be a service to the nation and the Reich.

5. Mr Churchill on Act of Surrender[5]

The Times, 9 May 1945

...Yesterday morning at 2.41 a.m. at headquarters, General Jodl, the representative of the German High Command, and of Grand Admiral Dönitz, the designated head of the German State, signed the act of unconditional surrender of all German land, sea, and air forces in Europe to the Allied Expeditionary Force, and simultaneously to the Soviet High Command. General Bedell Smith, Chief of Staff of the Allied Expeditionary Force, and General François Seve signed the document on behalf of the Supreme Commander of the Allied Expeditionary Force, and General Susloparov signed on behalf of the Russian High Command.

To-day this agreement will be ratified and confirmed at Berlin, where Air Chief Marshal Tedder, Deputy Supreme Commander of the Allied Expeditionary Force, and General de Lattre de Tassigny will sign on behalf of General Eisenhower. Marshal Zhukov will sign on behalf of the Soviet High Command. The German representatives will be Field-Marshal Keitel, Chief of the High Command and the Commanders-in-Chief of the German Army, Navy and Air Forces. Hostilities will end officially at one minute after midnight to-night (Tuesday, 8 May), but in the interests of saving lives the 'Cease fire' began yesterday to be sounded all along the front, and our dear Channel Islands are also to be freed to-day.

The Germans are still in places resisting the Russian troops, but should they continue to do so after midnight they will, of course, deprive themselves of the protection of the laws of war, and will be attacked from all quarters by the Allied troops. It is not surprising that on such long fronts and in the existing disorder of the enemy the commands of the German High Command should not in every case be obeyed immediately. This does not, in our opinion, with the best military advice at our disposal, constitute any reason for withholding from the nation the facts communicated to us by General Eisenhower of the unconditional surrender already signed at Reims, nor should it prevent us from celebrating to-day and to-morrow (Wednesday) as Victory in Europe days.

To-day, perhaps, we shall think mostly of ourselves. To-morrow, we shall pay a particular tribute to our Russian comrades, whose prowess in the field has been one of the grand contributions to the general victory. The German war is therefore at an end. After years of intense preparation, Germany hurled herself on Poland at the beginning of September 1939; and, in pursuance of our guarantee to Poland and in agreement with the French Republic, Great Britain, the British Empire and Commonwealth of nations [sic], declared war upon this foul aggression. After gallant France had been struck down we, from this island and from our united Empire, maintained the struggle single-handed for a whole year until we were joined by the military might of Soviet Russia and later by the overwhelming power and resources of the United States of America.

Finally, almost the whole world was combined against the evil-doers, who are now prostrate before us. Our gratitude to our splendid Allies goes forth from all our hearts in this island and throughout the British Empire. We may allow ourselves a brief period of rejoicing; but let us not forget for a moment the toil and efforts that lie ahead. Japan, with all her treachery and greed, remains unsubdued. The injury she has inflicted on Great Britain, the United States, and other countries, and her detestable cruelties, call for justice and retribution. We must now devote all our strength and resources to the completion of our task, both at home and abroad. Advance, Britannia! Long live the cause of freedom! God save the King!

NOTES

1. Public Record Office Kew, FO 371/46791, W.P. (45) 18.
2. Public Record Office Kew, FO 371/46864, C 257/257/18 (Series III).
3. From a selection of documents issued by Research Branch, Control Commission for Germany (British Element), Room 225, Norfolk House, St James's Square, London SW1 to all officers of the Control Commission (British Element), collection in toto dated 9 March 1945. Public Record Office Kew, FO 371/46864, C 952/257/18, HQ/2149 (Sec C), 1 March 1945, General.
4. Collection of Allied and German pronouncements relating to the final stages of the war in Europe, made by E.J. Passant, Foreign Office Research Department, Public Record Office Kew, FO 371/46785, C 2388/45/18, collection *in toto* dated 16 May 1945.
5. Public Record Office Kew, FO 371/46785, C 2388/45/18, Germany Confidential (16796), 9 May 1945.

8

Statistics

No claim is made that the statistics quoted here are undisputed. The situation at the time made the collection of data of this sort difficult and estimates vary according to source.

Table 1a German Bombs Dropped on Great Britain (tonnes)

Year	Tonnes
1940	36,800
1941	21,860
1942	3,260
1943	2,298
1944	9,151*
1945	761*

* including V-weapons.

Source: Der Große Ploetz. Auszug aus der Geschichte von den Anfängen bis zur Gegenwart, 31st edn (Würzburg, 1992), p 878.

STATISTICS

Table 1b Allied Bombs Dropped on Germany and Occupied Territories (tonnes)

1940	14,600
1941	35,500
1942	53,755
1943	226,500
1944	1,188,580
1945	477,000

Source: Der Große Ploetz. Auszug aus der Geschichte von den Anfängen bis zur Gegenwart, 31st edn (Würzburg, 1992), p 909.

Table 2 War Casualties

Country	Total	Civilians
Germany	5.25 million	500,000
Soviet Union*	20.6 million	7 million
USA	259,000	
Great Britain	386,000	62,000
France	810,000	470,000
Poland	4.52 million**	4.2 million
Italy	330,000	
Romania	378,000	
Hungary	420,000	280,000
Yugoslavia	1.69 million	1.28 million
Finland	84,000	
Norway	10,000	
Denmark	1,400	
Bulgaria	20,000	
Greece	160,000	140,000
Belgium	88,000	76,000
Netherlands	210,000	198,000
Japan	1.8 million	600,000
China	unknown	
Total	about 55 million	

* Official Soviet Union statistics.

** In addition, 1.5 million in the territories annexed by the Soviet Union in 1939.

Source: Der Große Ploetz. Auszug aus der Geschichte von den Anfängen bis zur Gegenwart, 31st edn (Würzburg, 1992), p 916.

Table 3a German Prisoners-of-War

Land	Total	Male	% male population	Female
Schleswig-Holstein	51,359	51,186	4.42	173
Hamburg	20,462	20,446	3.19	16
Lower Saxony	111,598	111,447	3.95	151
Nordrhein-Westfalen	206,789	206,569	3.90	220
British Zone	390,208	389,648	3.92	560

Source: Statistisches Amt für die Britische Besatzungszone Hauptabteilung D – Hamburg, 10 November 1947, Bundesarchiv Koblenz, BA 150/323, vol 2. Quoted from Arthur L. Smith, *Die 'vermißte Million'. Zum Schicksal deutscher Kriegsgefangener nach dem Zweiten Weltkrieg, Schriftenreihe der Vierteljahrshefte für Zeitgeschichte* 65 (Munich, 1992), p 124.

Table 3b Allied Prisoners-of-War

Occupying power	Total	Released
USA	30,976	planned: 15,873 in US Zone
Great Britain	435,295	monthly: 17,500; from 1 July: 20,000
France	631,483	
Soviet Union*	890,535	since capitulation: allegedly 1,003,974

* Official statistics according to Tass.

Source: Moscow Conference of Foreign Ministers, 10 March–24 April 1947, Official statistics, *Süddeutsche Zeitung*, no. 27, 18 March 1947. Quoted from Arthur L. Smith, *Die 'vermißte Million'. Zum Schicksal deutscher Kriegsgefangener nach dem Zweiten Weltkrieg, Schriftenreihe der Vierteljahrshefte für Zeitgeschichte* 65 (Munich, 1992), p 110.

Table 4 Missing Ex-Wehrmacht Members

Country	Total	1/1/45 to 8/5/45	9/5/45 to 31/12/45	1/1/46 and later
Germany*	12,724	10,617	191	115
Great Britain	332	95	8	9
USA	105	34	5	2
France	3,417	584	37	46
Poland	4,160	3,088	51	28
Romania	4,841	133	41	8
Italy	1,609	722	11	4
Yugoslavia	1,347	620	16	20
Soviet Union	45,693	8,790	267	312

* Territory of Occupied Zones.

Source: Bundesarchiv Koblenz, BA, Z 35/489. Quoted from Arthur L. Smith, *Die 'vermißte Million'. Zum Schicksal deutscher Kriegsgefangener nach dem Zweiten Weltkrieg, Schriftenreihe der Vierteljahrshefte für Zeitgeschichte* 65 (Munich, 1992), p 134.

Select Bibliography

Over the course of fifty years a number of general studies of the end of the Second World War and its place in German and international history have been presented. These wider-reaching accounts include the early and important work by Friedrich Meinecke, *Die deutsche Katastrophe* (1946), written under the immediate impact of the end of the war, and reach to recent publications such as Eric Hobsbawm's *Age of Extremes* (1995).

The analysis of the 1930s and 1940s in both Britain and Germany has been deepened continually by work on domestic policy, the public sphere, individual personalities and wide-reaching policies alike. In this context the work of Lothar Kettenacker (British war-time planning), Alan Bullock (Hitler), Ian Kershaw (propaganda in Nazi Germany), Martin Gilbert (Churchill), Anthony J. Nicholls (Weimar to Hitler) should be mentioned particularly.

While our knowledge of both broad developments and specific aspects of the pre-war and war years is expanding rapidly, the months around capitulation have not received detailed analysis by historians, a circumstance which reflects the scarcity of surviving records on the German side. Among the very few exceptions is Walter Lüdde-Neurath's study of the Dönitz government (1964).

This picture changes for the occupation period, which has been analysed by both German and British scholars, among them Donald C. Watt, Rolf Steiniger, Ulrich Reusch and Josef

Foschepoth. This is indeed an ever-widening area of research which increasingly draws on the records of the British Control Commission for Germany (British Element) in the Public Record Office, Kew. While the accent of this branch of scholarship falls on official records, there is a broad movement towards the inclusion of private individual records in the wider analysis, for example, letters and diaries of contemporaries. Access to this methodological approach can be gained via the works of R. Blythe, Wolfram Wette and S. zur Nieden, to name but a few. The select bibliography also contains some of the better known contemporary diaries, like Erich Kästner's *Notabene 1945*. Generally, this select bibliography aims to guide the reader to the topics raised in this volume: from preconceptions of the Germans in British public opinion (see, for example, Asa Briggs' and Anthony Nicholls' works), to concrete war-time planning (cf. Lothar Kettenacker's and Albrecht Tyrell's studies), to aspects of occupation policy. See, for example, the overview of British occupation policy from an 'official' point of view by Frank Donnison, and the analysis of specific and regional aspects by Wolfgang Jacobmeyer on displaced persons, Nicholas Pronay on re-education, and Kurt Jürgensen on British policy in Schleswig-Holstein. The source material for the British occupation authorities in Germany from 1944 to 1955 is accessible at the Public Record Office, Kew (see Adolf M. Birke and Eva A. Mayring, *Britische Besatzung in Deutschland. Aktenerschließung und Forschungsfelder*, published by the German Historical Institute London, London, 1992). Other relevant archival material can be found at the Imperial War Museum, London; the Bundesarchiv, Koblenz; and the Militärgeschichtliches Forschungsamt, Freiburg i.B.; as well as in the Bibliothek für Zeitgeschichte, Stuttgart. References to specific collections quoted and reproduced in extracts are given with the texts in the relevant chapters of the present volume.

I. Unpublished Sources

Public Record Office, Kew

Foreign Office General Correspondence
War Office Papers
War Cabinet Papers

Imperial War Museum, London
Department of Documents, Collection of Individual Papers
Photographic Department, Collection of Photographs

Bibliothek für Zeitgeschichte Stuttgart
Archivalische Sammlungen

II. Secondary Works and Published Sources

Adenauer, Konrad, *Erinnerungen 1945–53*, Stuttgart 1969.
Annan, Noel, *Changing Enemies. The Defeat and Regeneration of Germany*, London, 1995.
Balfour, Michael and John Mair, *Four Power Control in Germany and Austria 1945–1946*, Oxford, 1956.
Barker, Elisabeth, *The British between the Superpowers 1945–1950*, London, 1986.
Benz, Wolfgang, *Von der Besatzungsherrschaft zur Bundesrepublik. Stationen einer Staatsgründung 1946–1949*, Frankfurt, 1984.
Birke, Adolf, 'Warum Deutschlands Demokratie versagte, Geschichtsanalyse im britischen Außenministerium 1943/1945', *Historisches Jahrbuch* 103 (1983), pp 395–410.
Birley, Robert, *The German Problem and the Responsibility of Britain. The Burge Memorial Lecture*, SCM Press, London, 1947.
Blythe, R. (ed) *Private Words. Letters and Diaries from the Second World War*, London, 1993.
Bramwell, Anna C. (ed), *Refugees in the Age of Total War*, London, 1988.
Braunthal, Gerard, 'The Anglo-Saxon Model of Democracy: The West German Political Consciousness after World War II', *Archiv für Sozialgeschichte* 18 (1978), pp 245–77.
Bridgman, Jon, *The End of the Holocaust. The Liberation of the Camps*, London, 1990.
Briggs, Asa, *The War of Words: The History of Broadcasting in the United Kingdom*, vol III, London and Oxford, 1970.
Broszat, Martin, *The Hitler State. The Foundation and Development of the Internal Structure of the Third Reich*, London and New York, 1981.
Buchbender, O. and R. Sterz, *Das andere Gesicht des Krieges. Deutsche Feldpostbriefe 1939–1945*, Munich, 1982.
Bullock, Alan, *The Life and Times of Ernest Bevin, vol II, Minister of Labour. 1940–1945*, London, 1967.
Burridge, T.D., *British Labour and Hitler's War*, London, 1976.
Buttner, Ursula, 'Not nach der Befreiung. Die Situation der deutschen Juden in der britischen Besatzungszone 1945 bis 1948', *Das Unrechtsregime*, vol 2, *Verfolgung Exil-Belasteter. Neubeginn*, Hamburg, 1986.
Calder, A., *The Myth of the Blitz*, London, 1991.
Childers, Thomas and Jane Kaplan (eds), *Reevaluating the Third Reich*, New York and London, 1993.

BIBLIOGRAPHY

Churchill, Winston, *The Second World War*, vol 3, London, 1950.
Conze, Werner and M. Rainer Lepsius (eds), *Sozialgeschichte der Bundesrepublik Deutschland. Beiträge zum Kontinuitätsproblem*, Stuttgart, 1983.
Dalton, Hugh, *High Tide and After. Memoirs 1945–1960*, London, 1962.
Deist, W., M. Messerschmidt, H.-E. Volkmann and W. Wette, *Ursachen und Voraussetzungen des Zweiten Weltkrieges*, Frankfurt am Main, 1989.
Donnison, Frank S.V., *Civil Affairs and Military Government North-West Europe 1944–1946*, London, 1961.
Eade, Charles (ed), *The War Speeches of the Rt. Hon. Winston S. Churchill*, vol 3, London, 1962.
Eggebrecht, Axel, *Der halbe Weg. Zwischenbilanz einer Epoche*, Hamburg, 1981.
Ellis, J., *The Sharp End. The Fighting Man in World War I*, London, 1993.
Fest, Joachim C., *Hitler*, London, 1974.
Foschepoth, Josef and Rolf Steininger (eds), *Britische Deutschland- und Besatzungspolitik 1945–1949*, Paderborn, 1985.
Fussell, P., *Wartime. Understanding and Behavior in the Second World War*, New York and Oxford, 1989.
Gannon, F.R., *The British Press and Germany 1936–1939*, Oxford, 1971.
Gilbert, Martin, *Sir Horace Rumbold. Portrait of a Diplomat, 1869–1941*, London, 1973.
Grainger, J.H., *Patriotisms. Britain 1900–1939*, London, 1986.
Güstrow, Dietrich, *In jenen Jahren. Aufzeichnungen eines 'befreiten' Deutschen*, Munich, 1985.
Hammer, J. and S. zur Nieden (eds), *Sehr selten habe ich geweint. Briefe und Tagebücher aus dem Zweiten Weltkrieg von Menschen aus Berlin*, Zurich, 1992.
Hasenclever, Walter, *Ihr werdet Deutschland nicht wiedererkennen. Erinnerungen*, Munich, 1978.
Hildebrand, Klaus, *Das vergangene Reich. Deutsche Außenpolitik von Bismarck bis Hitler 1871–1945*, Stuttgart 1995.
——— 'Reich – Nation-State – Great Power. Reflections on German Foreign Policy 1871–1945', The 1993 Annual Lecture of the German Historical Institute London, London, 1995.
Hobsbawm, E.J., *Age of Extremes*, London, 1995.
Holtmann, Everhard, *Wie neu war der Neubeginn? Zum deutschen Kontinuitätsproblem nach 1945*, Erlangen, 1989.
Howard, Michael, *The Continental Commitment. The Dilemma of British Defence Policy Wars*, Harmondsworth, 1974.
Ingrams, Harold, 'Building Democracy in Germany', *The Quarterly Review* 285 (1947), pp 208–22.
Jacobmeyer, Wolfgang, *Vom Zwangsarbeiter zum heimatlosen Ausländer. Die Displaced Persons in Westdeutschland 1945–1951*, Göttingen, 1985.
James, Harold and Marla Stone (eds), *When the Wall Came Down. Reactions to German Unification*, London, 1992.
Jürgensen, Kurt, 'The Concept and Practice of Re-education', in N. Pronay and K. Wilson (eds), *The Political Re-education of Germany and Her Allies*, London, 1985.
——— 'British Occupation Policy after 1945 and the Problem of "Re-educating" Germany', *History* 68 (1983), pp 225–44.

Kantorowicz, Alfred, *Deutsches Tagebuch. Erster Teil*, Berlin, 1980.
Kästner, Erich, *Notabene 1945. Ein Tagebuch*, Munich, 1989.
Kennedy, Paul and Anthony J. Nicholls (eds), *Nationalist and Racialist Movements in Britain and Germany before 1914*, London, 1981.
Kershaw, Ian, *The 'Hitler Myth'. Image and Reality in the Third Reich*, Oxford, 1987.
Kessel, Martina, *Westeuropa und die deutsche Teilung. Englische und französische Deutschlandpolitik auf den Außenministerkonferenzen von 1945 bis 1947*, Munich, 1989.
Kettenacker, Lothar, 'Preußen in der alliierten Kriegszielplanung 1939–1947', in Lothar Kettenacker et al. (eds), *Studien zur Geschichte Englands und der deutsch-britischen Beziehungen. Festschrift für Paul Kluke*, Munich, 1981.
────── 'Die britische Haltung zum deutschen Widerstand während des Zweiten Weltkrieges', in Lothar Kettenacker (ed.), *The 'Other Germany' in the Second World War*, Stuttgart, 1977, pp 49–77 (includes English summary).
────── *Krieg zur Friedenssicherung. Deutschlandplanung der britischen Regierung während des Zweiten Weltkriegs*, Göttingen, 1989.
Krüger, Wolfgang, *Entnazifiziert? Zur Praxis der politischen Säuberung in Nordrhein-Westfalen*, Wuppertal, 1982.
Kulka, Otto D., 'Die deutsche Geschichtsschreibung über den Nationalsozialismus, und die "Endlösung" Tendenzen und Entwicklungsphasen 1924–1984', *Historische Zeitschrift* 240 (1985), pp 599–640.
Küsters, Hanns Jürgen and Hans Peter Mensing (eds), *Kriegsende und Neuanfang am Rhein. Konrad Adenauer in den Berichten des Schweizer Generalkonsuls Franz-Rudolph von Weiss 1944–1945*, Munich, 1986.
Longmate, N., *How We Lived Then. A History of Everyday Life During the Second World War*, London, 1973 (1st edn 1971).
Loth, Wilfried (ed), *Die deutsche Frage in der Nachkriegszeit*, Berlin, 1994.
Lüdde-Neurath, Walter, *Regierung Dönitz. Die letzten Tage des Dritten Reiches*, Göttingen, 1964.
Mammach, Klaus, *Der Volkssturm. Das letzte Aufgebot 1944/45*, Berlin, 1981.
Mansell, Gerard, *Let Truth be Told. 50 Years of BBC External Broadcasting*, London, 1982.
Marshall, Barbara, *The Origins of Post-War German Politics*, London, 1988.
Marwick, Arthur, *The Home Front. The British and the Second World War*, London, 1976.
────── *British Society Since 1945*, London, 1990.
Maschke, Erich (ed), *Zur Geschichte der deutschen Kriegsgefangenen des Zweiten Weltkriegs*, vol XV, Munich, 1974.
Michalka, Wolfgang (ed), *Das Dritte Reich*, vol 2, *Weltmachtanspruch und nationaler Zusammenbruch 1939–1945*, Munich, 1985.
Moggeridge, Donald (ed), *Maynard Keynes. Collected Writings*, London, 1980.
Moran, Lord, *Winston Churchill. The Struggle for Survival 1940–1965*, London, 1966.
Murawski, Erich, *Der deutsche Wehrmachtbericht 1939–1945*, Boppard/Rhein, 1962.
Overesch, Manfred, *Deutschland 1945–1949. Vorgeschichte und Gründung der Bundesrepublik. Ein Leitfaden in Darstellung und Dokumenten*, Düsseldorf, 1979.
Pakenham, Lord, *Born to Believe. An Autobiography*, London, 1953.

Paterson, William E., 'The British Labour Party and the SPD 1945-52', in *Kurt Schumacher als deutscher und europäischer Sozialist (Materialien zur politischen Bildungsarbeit)*, ed. Friedrich-Ebert-Stiftung, Bonn, 1988, pp 95-112.
Pimlott, Ben (ed), *The Second World War Diary of Hugh Dalton*, London, 1986.
Pocock, Tom, *1945: The Dawn Came Up Like Thunder*, London, 1983.
Pronay, Nicholas, 'Defeated Germany in British Newsreels: 1944-45', in K.R.M. Short and Stephen Dolezel (eds), *Hitler's Fall: The Newsreel Witness*, London, 1990.
Pronay, Nicholas and Keith Wilson (eds), *The Political Re-Education of Germany and Her Allies*, London, 1985.
Reusch, Ulrich, *Deutsches Berufsbeamtentum und britische Besatzung. Planung und Politik 1943-1947*, Stuttgart, 1985.
Rudzio, Wolfgang, 'Export englischer Demokratie? Zur Konzeption der britischen Besatzungspolitik in Deutschland', *Vierteljahrshefte für Zeitgeschichte* 17 (1969), pp 219-36.
Sanger, E., *Letters from Two World Wars. A Social History of English Attitudes towards War, 1914-1945*, London, 1993.
Scharf, Claus and Hans-Joachim Schröder (eds), *Die Deutschlandpolitik Großbritanniens und die britische Zone 1945-1949*, Wiesbaden, 1979.
Schikorsky, I., 'Kommunikation über das Unbeschreibbare. Beobachtungen zum Sprachstil von Kriegsbriefen', *Wirkendes Wort. Deutsche Sprache und Literatur in Forschung und Lehre* 2 (1992), pp 295-315.
Schlange-Schöningen, Hans, *Im Schatten des Hungers. Dokumentarisches zur Ernährungspolitik und Ernährungswirtschaft in den Jahren 1945-1949*, Hamburg, 1955.
Schneider, Ullrich, 'Grundzüge britischer Deutschland- und Besatzungspolitik', *Zeitgeschichte* 9 (1981/82), pp 73-89.
Schulze, Rainer, Doris von der Brelie-Lewien and Helga Grebing (eds), *Flüchtlinge und Vertriebene in der westdeutschen Nachkriegsgeschichte. Bilanzierung der Forschung und Perspektiven für die künftige Forschungsarbeit*, Hildesheim, 1987.
Schwarz, Angela, *Die Reise ins Dritte Reich. Britische Augenzeugen im nationalsozialistischen Deutschland (1933-39)*, Göttingen, 1993.
Schwarzwälder, Herbert, *Bremen und Nordwestdeutschland am Kriegsende 1945*, vol 2, *Der britische Vorstoß an die Weser*, Bremen, 1973.
Sharp, Tony, *The Wartime Alliance and the Zonal Division of Germany*, Oxford 1975.
Sherwood, Robert E., *The White House Papers of Harry L. Hopkins*, vol 2, London, 1949.
Sington, Derrick, *Belsen Uncovered*, London, 1947.
Smith, Anthony, *The British Press since the War*, London, 1974.
Smith, Arthur L., *Die 'vermißte Million'. Zum Schicksal deutscher Kriegsgefangener nach dem Zweiten Weltkrieg*, Schriftenreihe des Instituts für Zeitgeschichte, vol 65, Munich, 1992.
——— *Churchills deutsche Armee. Die Anfänge des Kalten Krieges*, Bergisch Gladbach, 1978.
Steininger, Rolf, *Deutsche Geschichte 1945-1961*, vol 1-2, Frankfurt am Main, 1983.
Treue, Wilhelm, 'Robert Pferdmenges (1880-1962)', *Geschichte im Westen* 2 (1990), pp 188-201.

Turner, Ian D. (ed), *Reconstruction in Post-War Germany. British Occupation Policy and the Western Zones*, Oxford, 1989.
Tyrell, Albrecht, *Großbritannien und die Deutschlandplanung der Alliierten 1941–1945*, Frankfurt am Main, 1987.
Vogel, Detlef and Wolfram Wette (eds), *Andere Helme – andere Menschen? Heimaterfahrung und Frontalltag im Zweiten Weltkrieg. Ein internationaler Vergleich*, Essen, 1995.
Watt, Donald C., *Britain Looks to Germany. British Opinion and Policy towards Germany since 1945*, London, 1965.
Wette, Wolfram (ed), *Der Krieg des kleinen Mannes. Eine Militärgeschichte von unten*, Munich and Zurich, 1992.
Woodward, Llewelyn, *British Foreign Policy in the Second World War*, London, 1962.
Wyman, Mark, *Europe's DPs 1945–1951*, Philadelphia, 1989.

Notes on Contributors

Lord Annan (Noel Gilroy Annan) served in the War Cabinet Offices and was a member of the Political Division of the Control Commission for Germany (British Element) in 1945–46. He has published widely in the fields of Victorian studies, the history of ideas and British–German relations in the twentieth century. Lord Annan is a former Vice-Chancellor of the University of London.

Ulrike Jordan is a Research Fellow at the German Historical Institute London. Her current area of work is British legal occupation policy in post-war Germany.

Kurt Jürgensen is Professor Emeritus at Christian-Albrechts-Universität, Kiel. His main field of work is post-1945 regional history, and he has published widely on British–German relations during the occupation years.

Lothar Kettenacker is Deputy Director of the German Historical Institute London and Professor of History at the University of Frankfurt am Main. He has published widely on the Third Reich and Anglo-German relations in the twentieth century.

Anthony J. Nicholls is a Fellow at the European Studies Centre, St Antony's College, Oxford. He has taught and published extensively on German political history and the history of ideas and mentalities in the nineteenth and twentieth centuries.

Otto Graf Lambsdorff is a former Economics Minister of the Federal Republic of Germany (1978–84). Since 1990, he has been Chairman of the Free Democratic Party in Germany. He has been active in numerous political and economic positions since the 1950s.

Peter von Zahn was in 1945 head of department of the North West German Radio (NWDR) in Hamburg (Wort und Kommentar); he went on to become political commentator for the NWDR in the USA (1951–60). He has subsequently pursued an active career in television broadcasting, writing and academic teaching.

Index

Act of Surrender 145
adaptability, speculations on German 134
Adenauer, Konrad 74–6, 78–80
administration, occupation policy 1, 58–9, 62
Ailwyn, Lord (Ailwyn Edward Fellowes) 46
Alexander, Frank 63
Allied Control Commission 6, 17–18, 46
Allied Expeditionary Force 145
Allied Supreme Command 2
American zone of occupation 79
Annan, Lord (Noel Annan) 69–70
announcements by German leaders, 1–8 May 1945 139f.
Antifa groups 73
appeasement 31
Ardennes offensive 3
Army Group (21), British Liberation Army 8
Army Welfare Service 63–4
Attlee, Clement 32, 35, 86
Auschwitz 80

Baden 118, 123
Balfour, Michael 61
Barbarossa, Emperor Friedrich 23
Barke, Lieutenant-General Evelyn 60
Bassum 105

Bavaria 117
Bayreuth 141
British Broadcasting Corporation (BBC) 7, 40–2
German Service 84
War Reports 40
Beaverbrook, Lord (William Maxwell Aitken) 41
Belgium 59
Ben-Gurion, David 80
Bergen-Belsen concentration camp 5, 9, 36, 64, 70, 80, 84, 87, 89, 92, 98
British reactions 95–6
documentary film 43, 93
food supply 96
Berlin 4, 6, 18–21, 36, 41, 63, 75, 94, 104, 110, 120
Berlin Blockade 76
Bevin, Ernest 34, 73–4, 86
Birley, Robert 54, 72
Bismarck, Otto von 7, 14, 21, 27
Blomberg, General Werner von 129
Böckler, Hans 73
Bolshevism 140
Borussianismus 128
Bracken, Brendan 32
Braun, Eva 4
Brecht, Bertolt 80
Bremervörde 91, 105
British Admiralty 19
British Army 5, 9

British Army of the Rhine (BOAR) 58
  Army Territorial Service 91
British camps 113
British Commonwealth 76, 146
British Control Group 83
British Empire 146
British Foreign Office 10, 16, 18–20, 23, 31, 38, 57, 73, 75
British media 3, 7, 40
British Military Government
  schools 59
  jurisdiction 91
British post-war planning 5, 13
British public opinion 7
British Royal Marines 81
British trade unions 44
British War Cabinet 70
British zone of occupation 21, 79
Buchenwald concentration camp 5, 26, 36, 80, 87
  documentary films 43, 93
Bundeswehr 79
Busch, General Ernst 19, 57
Bussche, Axel von dem 94
Butler, Nevile Montague 76
Buxtehude 91
Byrnes, James 86

capitulation 2–3, 9, 41–2
Carleton Greene, Hugh 83–4
Casablanca, Conference of 15
Christian Democratic Union (CDU) 74
cease-fire 146
censorship 84
Chamberlain, Joseph Austen 28
Chamberlain, Neville 31
Channel Islands 146
Churchill, Winston S. 14–21, 28, 31–2, 49, 57–8, 70, 76, 79, 99, 145
Clay, General Lucius D. 75
clichés 2
coal mining, occupation policy 78
coal production 84
Cold War 7, 21, 85–6
'collective guilt' 10, 45
Cologne 74, 141
communism, 124
community, speculations on new German 124
complexity, German 132–3

concentration camps 2, 10, 36, 42–3, 46, 63, 80, 87, 110
  British reaction 89
  German responsibility 90
constitution, 1871 German 27
contemporary correspondence and diaries 9, 87ff.
contemporary documents and broadcasts 114ff.
contemporary eyewitness accounts 9
Control Commission (post-1918) 127
Control Commission for Germany, British Element (CCG/BE) 47, 72, 74
  Handbook of Military Government 60
  Public Relations and Information Services Control Group 63
  Radio Section 84
Copenhagen 40
Cripps, Stafford 31
cult of false values, speculations on German 136
culture, occupation policy 37
currency reform (1948) 75

Dachau concentration camp 30
  documentary film 43
Dahrendorf, Walther 75
Daily Express 42–3, 45–7, 49
Daily Herald 34, 41, 44, 46
Daily Mail 29, 41, 43–4, 46–7, 49
Daily Mirror 41
Daily Telegraph 29, 41, 44, 48
Dalton, Hugh 32–3
Delmenhorst 109
demilitarization 7, 37, 79
democracy 9, 26, 64
  speculations on establishment in Germany 123
denazification 7, 60–1, 64, 71, 91
Denmark 55
destruction 1, 4, 120
  Coventry 70, 120
  Dresden 70
  Guernica 70
  Hamburg 70
  London 70
  Rotterdam 70
Deutsch–Englische Gesellschaft 73
Dickens, Charles 90

INDEX

disease 96
dislocation 87
disorientation 1–2, 103
Displaced Persons (DPs), occupation policy 63, 72
Dönitz, Grand Admiral Karl 4, 19, 47–8, 55, 57, 102, 139–40, 142, 144–5
Dönitz government 8, 20, 53, 56, 58
double personality, speculations on German 134
Dresden 79, 141
DNVP (German National People's Party) 28

East Germany 77
East Prussia 3, 56, 80
Ebert, Friedrich 47
Economic Consequences of Defeat 29
The Economist 35–7
Eden, Anthony 14, 16, 19–20, 23, 32, 76, 114
education, occupation policy 37, 54
Eggebrecht, Axel 84
Eichmann trial 80
Eisenhower, General Dwight D. 20, 78, 86, 146
Elbe (river) 10, 20
elections, occupation policy 72
emigration, German 116
émigrés 8, 16
employment 116
epidemics 88
Essen 120
Europe 126, 140–2, 146
European Union 79
evacuation 2
    German efforts 56
Evening Standard 49
extremist tendencies, speculations on German 133

fighting morale 2
First World War 6–7, 28–30, 37, 45, 47–8, 115
Flensburg 55–7, 63
food distribution 84
forced labour 91, 94, 97–8
Fortnightly Review 27
Fraenkel, Heinrich 34
France 70, 146

fraternization 6, 36, 60, 62, 78, 83, 91–2
Frederick the Great 48
French zone of occupation 79
Friedeburg, Admiral Hans-Georg von 4, 8, 53
Frings, Cardinal Joseph (Archbishop of Cologne) 78
Fritzsche, Hans 111
fuel 116
Führer cult 8, 45
future alliances, predictions 119

Galen, Cardinal Clemens August von (Bishop of Münster) 73
Garvin, J.L. 48
Gaulle, Charles de 76
GDR 80
Gedye, G.E.R. 29–30
Geneva Convention 46
George VI, King of England 64
German Air Force 131
German Army 5, 31, 49, 117, 127
German broadcasting 103
German correspondence and diaries 100
German culture 20
German defeat, British reactions 92, 97
German Emperor 15, 128
German Empire (1871–1918) 28, 128
German High Command 16, 55–6, 58, 146
German historiography 23
German mentality 2, 7, 22, 42, 45, 49, 93, 114–5
German Navy 48
German officer mentality 10, 127
German officer, Nazi concept of 131
German post-surrender work discipline 105
German Reactions to Defeat (Foreign Office Memorandum) 35, 115
German reactions to defeat 2, 10, 222
German Reich government 4
German Social Democrats in exile 32
German surrender
    children's reactions 99
    civilian reactions 88, 98
German unification (1871) 27
German–Danish border 55

Gillies, Frank 32
Goebbels, Joseph 3, 18, 23, 48
Goering, Hermann 48, 121
Görlitz 194
Göttingen 101
Göttingen University 101
Greenwood, Arthur 34
Grigg, James 36, 71
Grotewohl, Otto 75
Guelph dynasty 27

Habsburg dynasty 27
Hamburg 74–5, 83, 91–2, 104–5
  Four Seasons Hotel 92
Hanseatic cities 123
Harpstedt 105
Harris, Air Marshal Arthur
harvesting 84
Harvey, Oliver 57
Henderson, Neville 31
Henderson, Brigadier Patrick 60–2
Hesse 77
Hildebrand, Klaus 23
Himmler, Heinrich 41
Historikerstreit 70
Hitler, Adolf 2–4, 6, 13–20, 22–3,
  28–9, 31, 36, 41–2, 45, 47, 77, 83,
  102–3, 116, 122, 139
  popular mandate 30
'Hitler myth' 2, 45
Hitler Youth 4, 16
'Hitlerism' 94, 123
Hoevermann, Otto 61–2
Hohenzollern monarchy 15, 27, 48
Holland 55, 59, 90
Holocaust 70, 80
honour, German officer's concept of
  130
Hopkins, Harry 21
Horrocks, General Brian G. 91
House of Commons 34–6. 130
House of Lords 43, 46, 54
Hull, Cordell 14
Huxley, Julian 34

Imperial Army 127
India 21
indirect rule 6, 9
indoctrination 2
industry, dismantling policy 78
infrastructure 1

Instrument of Unconditional
  Surrender 53–5
International Student Service 44

Japan 86
Jewish academics, expulsion 32
Jewish claims 80
Jews, mass murder 42
Joad, C.E.M. 34
Jodl, General Alfred 4, 145
Jowitt, Viscount (William Allan Jowitt)
  54

Keitel, Field Marshal Wilhelm 4,
  146
Ketteler, Emmanuel (Bishop of Mainz)
  127
Keynes, John Maynard 13, 29, 71
Kiel 55, 60–1, 64, 81
  Kiel Canal 40
  Kiel University 62
Kinzel, General Eberhard 57
Kirkpatrick, Ivone 65
Klein Hesepe (village) 90
Koeppler, Heinz 72
Königswinter conferences 73
KPD (German Communist Party)
  75
Kronberg 104
Kurland (Latvia) 81

Labour Party, British 32–4
Labour Service 131
Lambsdorff, Count Otto von 69
land reform 78
Laski, Harold 34
Lattre de Tassigny, General Jean de
  146
League of Nations 49
liberalism 22, 27
Lingen 90
Lithuania 56
London 120
'lost generations', speculations 123
Lübeck 63, 94
Lüneberg 97

Mark Brandenburg 100
Marshall Plan 79
Milch, Erhard 131
Milchsach, Lilo 73

INDEX

militarism 6–7, 15, 20, 28, 31–2, 48, 59, 64, 121–3, 125–6
Military Courts 64
modernization 17
Molotov, Vojcheslav Mikhailovich 14
Montgomery, Field Marshal Bernard Law 4, 37, 49, 53–7, 60, 64, 78, 83, 86, 90
Moorehead, Alan 49
morale, German 2
Morgenthau Plan 34, 71, 79
Moscow 14, 57
Munich 28, 30
Munich Agreement (1938) 71
Munster, Lord (Geoffrey W.R.H. FitzClarence) 46
music, German 27
Mussolini, Benito 29

Nathan, Lord (Harry Louis Nathan) 54
nation-state 13
National Union of Distributive and Allied Workers 44
'national character' 7, 9, 21, 26, 132
nationalism 21
    German 123
    speculations on resurgence 125
NATO 79, 81
Nazi elite 2
Nazi–Soviet Pact 75
Neuengamme camp 91
New Statesman 42
News Chronicle 40–1
Nijmegen 90
Noel-Baker, Philip 34
Nordwestdeutscher Rundfunk 73, 83, 85
Normandy Campaign 95
Northcliffe, Lord (Alfred Harmsworth) 41
northern Germany 6, 8, 55
Nuremberg 141
Nuremberg trials 80

O'Neill, Con 22–3, 35–6
occupation policy 1, 6
occupation 6, 15, 53
Oder-Neiße line 80
Ohne mich movement 81
Ollenhauer, Erich 33

pacifism 116
Pantos, Selkin 45
Papen, Franz von 17
perception of the enemy 87
Petersen, Rudolf 74
Poe, Edgar Allan 90
Poland 21, 125, 146
political camps 89
political parties, re-establishment 74
political prisoners 88, 95
postal services 5
Potsdam Agreement 71, 74
Prague, Jewish camp 102
prisoners of war (POWs) 5, 8, 10, 42, 46, 72, 77, 83, 94–5, 106
POW camps 89, 97, 105
progress, speculations on 126
propaganda 2–3, 5, 72, 84, 87, 110
Prussia 16, 28, 59, 118, 127–8
psychological change 2
psychological stress 87
public service 3

racism 37
Radio Hamburg 83
Ramsey, Guy 47
Randall, Leslie 49
Rangoon 40
rape 97
Rauschnigg, Hermann 30
re-education 7–8, 21, 35–8, 44
Reading, Lord (Gerald Rufus Reading) 46–7
Red Army 5, 19–20, 77, 81, 86, 111
refugees 4, 21, 42, 47, 79, 92, 104
regard for authority, speculations on German 137
Reichenau, Major-General Walter von 129
Reichstag elections, March 1933 30
Reichswehr 94
Reims 4, 146
reparations 71
repression, speculations on German 138
resistance 2
retribution 44
Rhineland 117, 123
Ribbentrop, Joachim von 14, 20, 45, 48

Riddy, Donald (Director of Education Branch, CCG/BE) 61–2, 64
Ritter, Gerhard 17
Robertson, General Brian 65
Roosevelt, Franklin D. 21, 23
Rothermere, Lord (Harold Sidney Harmsworth) 29
Rothfels, Hans 17
Rowse, A.L. 33
Royal Cadet College 127
Rudzio, Wolfgang 64
Ruhr area 21
Rumbold, Horace 29–30
Rundstedt Offensive (December 1944) 35

Sandbostel camp 5, 10, 87, 89–90, 105
   German schoolgirls work in 106
   situation of inmates 106
Sargent, Orme 20–1, 31, 57
Saturday Review 42
Saxony 102, 118
Schacht, Hjalmar 17
Schindler's List 80
Schleswig 60
Schleswig-Holstein 9, 19, 53, 55–6, 58–9, 61, 63, 77–8, 91
Schnitzler, Karl-Eduard von 83
Schulenberg, Gräfin Elisabeth von der 70
Schumacher, Kurt 33, 75
Schwerin von Krosigk, Conrad (German Foreign Minister) 20, 56, 140, 142, 144
Second World War 7, 10, 13, 15, 26, 31, 41, 47, 69, 79
SED (Socialist Unionist Party) 75
sense of inferiority, speculations on German 137
separatist movements, German 117
Seve, General François 145
Seyss-Inquart, Arthur 95
Siegfried Line 100
Silverman, Sidney 43
Smith, General Walter Bedell 145
Soltau-Celle 98
Soviet Army 79
Soviet High Command 145
Soviet Union 14–5, 17, 21, 23, 35, 55, 74–5, 79, 116, 118–9, 125, 146

SPD (German Socialist Party) 74–5
Special Operations Executive (SOE) 32
The Spectator 26, 36–7, 42
Spielberg, Steven 80
SS 88, 96–7, 106
stab-in-the-back legends 48–9
Stalin, Josef 6, 14
standard of life 126
   collapse in 116
Stanhope, Lord (James Richard Stanhope) 44
starvation 96
Steel, Christopher (Chief of Political Division, CCG/BE) 57, 61
Steltzer, Theodor 61–2
stereotypes 7, 29, 49, 81
Strander Bucht 81
Stumpff, Hans-Jürgen 4
subjectivity, speculations on German 135
Sudetenland 117
Supreme Headquarters Allied Expeditionary Force 57–8
supreme authority 1
surrender 77
   German reactions 103
   of Berlin, civilian reactions 111
   German High Command 142
Susloparov, General Ivan 145
Sweden 75
Sybel, Heinrich von 27

Taylor, A.J.P 41
Tedder, Air Chief Marshal Arthur William 145–6
Tehran Conference 85
Templer, General Gerald 64, 71, 73
The Times 20, 41, 56
Theresienstadt 80
Thoma, General Wilhelm von 20
Thuringia 77, 102
Torgau 4, 41
Trades Union Congress 33
transport 116
Treasury 17
treatment of civilians 88
Treaty of Rome (1957) 76
Treitschke, Heinrich von 28
Tribune 31

INDEX

Truman, Harry H. 86
20 July 1944 (attempt to assassinate Hitler) 17
typhus 96

Ulbricht, Walter 75
unconditional surrender 1, 5–6, 10, 15, 40, 55, 86
United Nations 79
   establishment of 141
United States 15, 76, 146–7
   US Loans to Britain 21, 71
Vandenhoeck & Ruprecht 102
Vansittart, Robert 16, 22, 31, 37, 43, 49
   Black Record 34
VE-Day 40, 56, 96, 146
Versailles Treaty 13, 15, 29–30, 71, 115, 129–30
victory 40
victory celebrations 99
VJ-Day 64
Vogel, Hans 33
Volkssturm (People's Army) 4, 100
Vorden 90

war aims 14, 28
war criminals, categorization 57
war guilt 84
wartime planning 6, 35

wartime analysis 2
Weertzen 91
Wehrmacht 6, 9, 101
   Northern German Army Group 94
Weimar 26
Weimar Republic 7, 28–30
   culture 71
Werewolf resistance movements 2
West Germany 3
Western Europe 119
Western Front (1914–18) 29
Wildeshausen 105
Wilhelm II 45
Wilton Park Centre 72
Woodward, Llewellyn 15
World Jewish Congress 43
WRNS (Women's Royal Navy Service) 91
Wünsdorf 129

xenophobia 37

Yalta Conference 35, 77

Die Zeit 73
Zeven 91
Zhukov, Marshal Grigory Konstantinovich 146
Zurich 79

www.ingramcontent.com/pod-product-compliance
Lightning Source LLC
Chambersburg PA
CBHW052046300426
44117CB00012B/1989